Modern Collectible Dolls

IDENTIFICATION
&
VALUE GUIDE

Patsy Moyer

COLLECTOR BOOKS

A Division of Schroeder Publishing Co., Inc.

The current values in this book should be used only as a guide. They are not intended to set prices, which vary from one section of the country to another. Auction prices as well as dealer prices vary greatly and are affected by condition as well as demand. Neither the Author nor the Publisher assumes responsibility for any losses that might be incurred as a result of consulting this guide.

Searching for a Publisher?
We are always looking for knowledgeable people considered to be experts within their fields. If you feel that there is a real need for a book on your collectible subject and have a large comprehensive collection, contact Collector Books.

On the Cover:
Left: 13½" Effanbee "Patsy," $400.00, Courtesy McMasters Auction
Bottom: 18" Shirley Temple, $950.00, Courtesy Angie Gonzales
Right: 23" Madame Alexander "McGuffey Ana," $2,100.00,
Courtesy McMasters Auction

Cover design: Beth Summers
Book design: Sherry Kraus

Additional copies of this book may be ordered from:

COLLECTOR BOOKS
P.O. Box 3009
Paducah, Kentucky 42002–3009

@ $19.95. Add $2.00 for postage and handling.

Copyright: Patsy Moyer, 1997

Contents

Dedication

Dedicated with love and affection to my husband, Dick Moyer, and grandchildren, Lisa and Chad Moyer, and Ryan and Becky Ramsey.

Credits

*My special thanks to the following people
who helped with photos and more:*

Vickie Applegate
Shirlijean Abel
Gay Baron
Millie Busch
Millred E. Carol
Hank Collins
Marjory Collins
Dee Cermak
Cathie Clark
Barbara Comienski
Patsy Corrigan
Barbara Cresenze
Debbie Crume
Barbara DeFeo
Rosemary Dent
Dee Domroe
Dorothy Doring
Elizabeth Dorsey
Jan Drugan
Susan Dunham
Jacquie Duran
Rose Endrusick
June Friel

Betty Fronefield
Marie Gardyne
Sondra Gast
Cherie Gervais
Angie Gonzales
June Goodnow
Shirley Grime
Irene Grundvig
Diane Gulomo
Betty Haddix
Amanda Hash
Patti Hale
Georgia Henry
Janet Hill,
Linda Holton
Sylvia Kleindinst
Sharon Kolibaba
Iva Mae Jones
Sue Kinkade
Lucia Kirsch
Joy Kramer
Jacquie Litchfield
Margaret Long

Louise M. Lunde
Helen Magill
Joyce Maloney
Margie's Doll House
Connie Lee Martin
Pamela Martinec
Matrix
Candy McCain
McMasters Doll
  Auctions
Sally McVey
Diane Miller
Pidd Miller
Peggy Millhouse
Bev Mitchell
Marilyn Moran
Peggy Montei
Carol Murphy,
Dorisanne Osborn
Elaine Pardee
Marian Pettygrove
Teri Pierce

Stephanie Prince
Marilyn Ramsey
Rosalie Whyel
  Museum of Doll Art
Pat Schuda
Eleanor Selmer
Barbara Schletzbaum
Trish Sheppard
Sherryl Shirran
Pat Smith
Mary Lee Stallings
Linda Lee Sutton
Martha Sweeney
Mary Lee Swope
Ann Tuma
Dorothy Vaughn
Virginia Vinton
Lorrie Wade
Margie Welker
Sue Wilkins
Toni Winder
Oleta Woodside.

Introduction

Perhaps "modern" is a misnomer for dolls over seventy years old and still considered by doll collectors to be modern. One factor influencing this, however, is that some companies that made dolls at the turn of the century are still operating and producing dolls. For this book, I am grouping dolls made of composition, cloth, rubber, hard plastic, porcelain, vinyl, wood, and some other materials as modern as opposed to dolls of bisque, wax, wood, and china that were made before and after World War I. There are no easy cut-off dates and some spill over from one category to the next. This book will give examples of dolls to compare for identification.

Collectors wanting to know more about the dolls they have or wanting to begin a collection, need to learn as much as possible. One way to do this is to research and arm yourself with books and magazines that deal with the subject. Another way is to seek other informed collectors. Beginning collectors may find it helpful to list their dolls with the prices paid, the size, marks, material, and other pertinent facts, such as originality and condition. Collectors need to be able to identify their dolls and one way to do this is by the material of which it is made.

One very basic thing beginning doll collectors need to understand is that experienced doll collectors refer to a doll by whatever material is used for making the doll's head. So a composition doll has a composition head but may have a cloth, composition, or wood body. A doll with a vinyl head and a hard plastic body is a vinyl doll. The head commands the order of reference to the doll in relation to materials used to produce it. A doll made entirely of vinyl is referred to as all vinyl. The doll may be described as being vinyl correctly when the body may be made of cloth, rubber, or hard plastic.

When collectors find a doll they wish to identify with no packaging or box, they first need to examine the back of the head, and then the torso and the rest of the body — the usual places manufacturers place their marks. Some dolls will only have a mold number or no mark at all. Nursing students are often given the task of writing a physical description of their patient starting at the top of their head down to the bottom of their feet. This way of looking at a doll to describe them and their attire is also a good procedure.

Collectors like to meet and network with other collectors sharing their interests. For this reason we have included a Collectors' Network section in the back of this book. There are many who belong to special interest groups that focus on one area of doll collecting. These are experienced collectors in a certain area who will network with others. It is considered proper form to send a SASE when contacting others if you wish to receive a reply. If you wish to be included in this area, please send your area of expertise and references.

In addition, a national organization, the United Federation of Doll Clubs has information for doll collectors who are seeking or wish to form a doll club. The goals of this non-profit organization focus on education, research, preservation, and enjoyment of dolls. They also sponsor a junior membership for budding doll collectors. They will put you in contact with one of 16 regional directors who will be able to assess your needs and advise you if a doll club in your area is accepting

Introduction

members.

You may write for more information to:

UFDC
10920 North Ambassador Drive
Suite 130
Kansas City, MO 64153
or FAX 816 891-8360

Beginning collectors, who have not recently won a lottery, may want to learn as much as possible about dolls before spending their money. Most collectors have to budget and do not have unlimited funds. It seems prudent to investigate thoroughly all avenues regarding an addition to one's collection before actually making a purchase.

Novice collectors may wonder where they can find dolls to buy. There are many different ways to locate the doll of your dreams, including finding dealers or shops that specialize in trying to locate a particular doll for you. There are numerous focus groups that list special sales and where they are being held. Collector groups usually post doll shows and sales in their newsletters.

Auctions may also prove to be an aid in finding additions to your collection. Some offer absentee bidding which is most helpful if you do not live near where the auction is being held. Some also offer over the phone bidding if you want to be able to be in on the actual bidding. Auction houses usually send out catalogs and answer questions over the phone or FAX if you need more information. See Collectors' Network at the back of this book for more information.

A simple easy way to keep track of the money spent on doll collections is to utilize a money program on your computer, using a number and description to keep track of your doll, then entering the amount you spend when purchasing it. If you sell the doll or dispose of it, it can be checked during the reconciling procedure and thus will not be seen when you wish to see a list of your current inventory. This is just a very simple way to help you with your doll inventory.

With time, collectors interests vary, but playthings remain a consistently enjoyable hobby for collectors. This book does not mean to set prices and should only be used as one of many tools to guide the collector. It is the collector's decision alone on which doll to purchase. It is the responsibility of the collector alone to choose his own area of collecting and how to pursue it. This book is meant to help you enjoy and learn about dolls of our past and present and give indications of various resources available to the thoughtful collector of the trends of the future.

Advertising Dolls

Manufacturing companies often use dolls as a means of advertising their products — either as a premium or in the form of a trademark of their company. Sometimes the dolls were given as a premium or as a reward for subscriptions to a magazine. This entrepreneurial spirit has given us some delightful examples and can bring a whole new realm of discovery for the collector. The advertising doll has been around since the late 1800s and continues to be a viable form of advertising. Advertising dolls now can be made just for the collector as a product themselves — look at the Christmas ornaments that advertise Barbie, space adventurers, and the McDonald's premiums in their children's Happy Meal boxes.

All these dolls or figurines that promote a product or service are called advertising dolls. Early companies that used dolls to promote their products were Amberg with Vanta Baby, American Cereal Co. with Cereta, American Character with the Campbell Kids, Buster Brown Shoes with Buster Brown, Ideal with Cracker Jack Boy and ZuZu Kid, Kellogg's with a variety of characters, and many others.

22" all rubber, reported to be an advertisement for Scotch whiskey. $150.00.
Courtesy Carol Murphy.

Advertising Dolls

Doll in Scottish dress was an advertising premium for Nabisco Wheat Honeys. $45.00. *Courtesy of Cathie Clark.*

"Aida, Toe Dancing Ballerina Doll" for "Capezio, the dancer's cobbler since 1887." $150.00. *Courtesy Cathie Clark.*

11½" vinyl, "Texaco Cheerleader," posable with wardrobe, British Crown Colony, Hong Kong, circa 1970s. $75.00. *Courtesy Cathie Clark.*

24" cloth, "Miss Korn-Krisp,"
marked on body: "My name is Miss Korn-Krisp,"
circa 1900. $225.00.
Courtesy Sherryl Shirran.

13½" printed cloth doll advertising
Kellogg's Corn Flakes and Pep. $150.00.
Courtesy Sharon Kolibaba.

Alexander Doll Company

Beatrice and Rose Alexander began the Alexander Doll Co. in about 1912. They were known for doll costumes and began using the "Madame Alexander" trademark in 1928. Beatrice A. Behrman became a legend in the doll world with her long reign as the head of the Alexander Doll Company. Alexander made cloth, composition, and wood dolls, and after World War II they made the transition to hard plastic and then into vinyl. The doll world was shocked this past year with skyrocketing prices paid at auction for some wonderful collectible Alexander dolls, including $56,000.00 for an 8" hard plastic doll re-dressed as the Infante of Prague. Alexander's rare and beautiful mint dolls continue to attract young collectors.

One of the Alexander company's luckiest breaks came when they obtained the exclusive license to produce the Dionne Quintuplet dolls in 1934. The Alexander Dionne Quintuples were introduced in 1935, and were made in both cloth and composition, as babies and toddlers. Some of the rarer groups are the bathtub set and sets with the wooden playground accessories like the carousel or Ferris wheel. Other companies tried to fill out their lines with sets of five identical dolls even though this brought copyright suits from Madame Alexander. Quintuplet collectors collect not only dolls, but clothing, photographs, and a large assortment of other related memorabilia. *Quint News* is published quarterly by Jimmy and Fay Rodolfos, founders of a nonprofit group:

Dionne Quint Collectors
PO Box 2527
Woburn MA 01888
$10.00 a year

Left: 15" cloth, Madame Alexander "Beth," tagged dress, $300.00.

Right: 16" "Amy," original dress, $350.00.

Courtesy McMasters Doll Auctions.

**20" hard plastic, Madame Alexander
"Cissy," boxed, $275.00.**
Courtesy McMasters Doll Auctions.

Left: 13" "Nurse," $825.00.

**Middle: 7½" composition, Madame Alexander
"Dionne Quintuplets," contained in original suitcase
with extra organdy dresses, $3,800.00.**

Right: 14" "Dr. Dafoe," $1,400.00.
Courtesy McMasters Doll Auctions.

**20" hard plastic, Madame Alexander
"Queen" (Cissy face), boxed, $825.00.**
Courtesy McMasters Doll Auctions.

**20" vinyl, Madame Alexander "Cissy," all original
in lavender and purple outfit, $550.00.**
Courtesy Sally McVey.

Alexander Doll Company

**13" composition, Madame Alexander
"Jeannie Walker," $1,200.00.**
Courtesy McMasters Doll Auctions.

**21" vinyl, Alexander "Judy" (Jacqueline),
with trunk and wardrobe, sold by FAO
Schwarz, 1962, $1,900.00.**
Courtesy McMasters Doll Auctions.

**14" hard plastic, Alexander
Little Women "Beth," with Fashion
Academy Award Tag, modern, $350.00.**
Courtesy Angie Gonzales.

**14" hard plastic, Madame Alexander "Little Women,"
original tagged outfits, $750.00.**
Courtesy McMasters Doll Auctions.

**14" hard plastic, Alexander "Little Women Set,"
all orignal, $1,500.00.**
Courtesy Angie Gonzales.

**14" hard plastic, Alexander Little Women
"Amy," with Fashion Academy Award Tag,
modern, $350.00.**
Courtesy Angie Gonzales.

**15" all composition, Madame Alexander
"Kate Greenaway," all original, $675.00.**
Courtesy Sherryl Shirran.

**21" vinyl, Madame Alexander "Mary
Mine," with cloth body, tagged clothes,
circa 1977, $150.00.**
Courtesy Angie Gonzales.

Alexander Doll Company

20" composition, Madame Alexander twin "McGuffey Anas," $675.00.
Courtesy Amanda Hash.

23" composition, Madame Alexander "McGuffey Ana," $2,100.00.
Courtesy McMasters Doll Auctions.

15" vinyl, Madame Alexander "Pollyanna," tagged dress, $330.00.
Courtesy McMasters Doll Auctions.

15" hard plastic, Madame Alexander "Nina Ballerina," tagged dress, $300.00.
Private Collection.

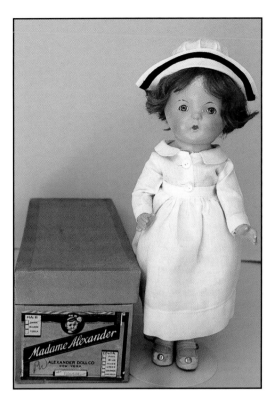

**13" composition, Madame Alexander "Nurse,"
all original with original box, circa 1935, blue
tin eyes, dress with cloth tag,
"Madame/Alexander/NY," $800.00.**
Courtesy Sherryl Shirran.

**Set of six 14" all vinyl, Madame Alexander "President's Wives,"
tagged fancy dresses, boxed, circa 1979, $900.00, set.**
Courtesy Angie Gonzales.

**13" Alexander "Princess Elizabeth," with
extra original wardrobe and case, $2,300.00.**
Courtesy McMasters Doll Auctions.

**18" vinyl, Madame Alexander "Pussy Cat,"
with cloth body, all original with box and
tag, circa 1977, $150.00.**
Courtesy Angie Gonzales.

Alexander Doll Company

Madame Alexander's "Scarlett," in long green
velveteen long coat and hat over plaid dress,
$1,300.00.
Courtesy Amanda Hash.

18" composition, Madame Alexander
"Snow White," all original, $600.00.
Courtesy Dee Domroe.

24" cloth, Madame Alexander
"So Lite Cloth Doll," $625.00.
Courtesy McMasters Doll Auctions.

16" cloth, Madame Alexander "Tiny Tim,"
circa 1923 – 1930, molded mask face of
flocked fabric, cloth tag on jacket, $725.00.
Courtesy Sherryl Shirran.

American Character

American Character Doll Co. (1919+, New York City) first made composition dolls. In 1923 they began using Petite as a tradename for mama and character dolls. They later made cloth, hard plastic, and vinyl dolls. American Character "Toni" dolls from the late 1950s are an interesting reflection of society's acceptance of women and girls focusing on primping and beauty, concentrating on hair. "Which twin has the Toni" ad campaigns and dolls used to advertise Toni Permanent Waves were common to the era. Toni, Sweet Sue, Tressy, Mary Make-up, and other dolls with high heels and fashion-type figures all reflect the idea of women as objects of beauty that remains an on-going theme in dolls.

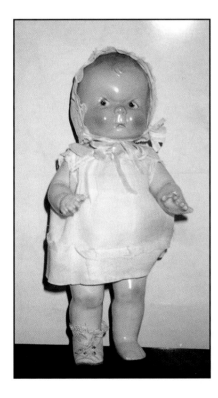

12" "Puggy," in tagged white dress and bonnet, marked on torso, "A PETITE DOLL," $450.00.

Courtesy Janet Hill.

13" and 15" American Character "Tiny Tears," hard plastic head, rubber body, original outfits, circa 1950, $150.00 – 175.00.

Courtesy Angie Gonzales.

American Character

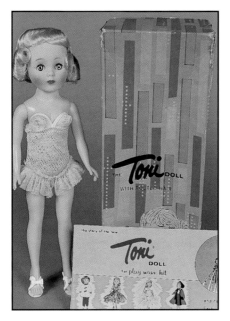

**10" vinyl, American Character
"Toni," $185.00.**
Courtesy McMasters Doll Auctions.

**14" hard plastic, American Character
"Annie Oakely," $325.00.**
Courtesy McMasters Doll Auctions.

**19" vinyl, American Character Whimsie
doll, "Fanny, the Flapper," circa 1960,
$95.00.**
Courtesy Cathie Clark.

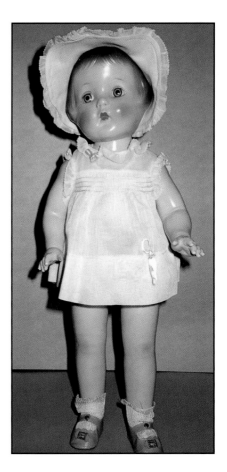

**21" composition, American Character
"Petite Sally," $350.00.**
Courtesy Irene Grundtvig.

"Tiny Tears," MIB, $300.00.
Courtesy Cathie Clark.

"Tiny Tears," with rockabye eyes,
as you rock her to sleep, her eyes close, $250.00.
Courtesy Cathie Clark.

21" vinyl, American Character
"Toni Play Wave," NRFB, $400.00.
Courtesy Irene Grundtvig.

16" vinyl, American Character
"Toni Play Wave," NRFB, $300.00.
Courtesy Irene Grundtvig.

American Character

Hard plastic "Sweet Sue" Bride by American Character, all original, tagged, $325.00.
Courtesy Cathie Clark.

Tagged "Sweet Sue"
by American Character, $300.00.
Courtesy Cathie Clark.

19" vinyl, American Character Whimsie doll, "Dixie the Pixie," circa 1960, $95.00.
Courtesy Cathie Clark.

Louis Amberg & Sons

Louis Amberg and Sons began in 1878 in Cincinnati, OH. From 1898 on they were located in New York City. They were known by other names before 1907. Amberg imported dolls made by other firms. They were one of the first manufacturers to produce all American-made dolls in quantities and were using a cold press composition as early as 1911. Their early dolls had cold press composition heads with straw stuffed bodies and composition lower arms. In 1915 they introduced a character doll, Charlie Chaplin, and he was a big hit for them. In 1918 Otto Denivelle joined the firm and introduced a hot press baking process for making composition dolls. Mibs, a soulful composition child with molded hair and painted eyes, was introduced in 1921. Soon Amberg and Sons were making Mama dolls and Baby Peggy. In 1927, they introduced the Vanta baby, which promoted Vanta baby clothing. In 1928 Amberg patented a waist joint and used several different heads on this body twist torso, one of which was called the It doll. In 1930, Amberg was sold to Horsman who continued to make some of the more popular lines.

**Left: 18" composition, Amberg "Vanta Baby,"
tagged diaper, shoulder plate, cloth body, $225.00.**
Courtesy McMasters Doll Auctions.

13" composition head, painted features,
cloth body, cloth tag on coat sleeve,
$450.00+.
Courtesy Debbie Crume.

Amberg body twist "It" doll,
composition, with box, $300.00.
Courtesy Cathie Clark.

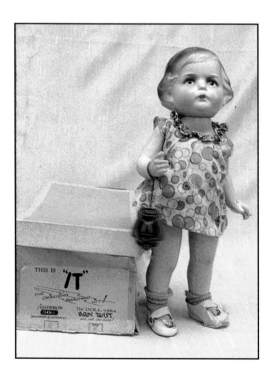

Arranbee

Arranbee Doll Co. was located in New York from 1922 until 1958. It was sold to Vogue Doll Co. who used its molds until 1961. Some of their bisque dolls were made by Armand Marseille and Simon & Halbig. They made composition baby, child, and mama dolls. Early dolls have an eight-sided tag. They went on to make hard plastic and vinyl dolls, many using the R&B trademark. Some hard plastic and vinyl dolls (Littlest Angel and Li'l Imp) were made for Vogue by the Arranbee division and may be marked by either.

**18" hard plastic "Darling Daisy Bride,"
with paper tag, $300.00.**
Courtesy Joyce Maloney.

Arranbee

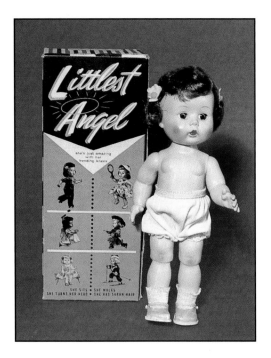

10½" "Littlest Angel,"
with box, original, $55.00.
Courtesy Angie Gonzales.

Left: 17" hard plastic "Nanette,"
original dress, $250.00.

Right: 15" Effanbee "Tintair Doll,"
with wrist tag, original dress, $250.00.
Courtesy McMasters Doll Auctions.

16" composition "Nancy,"
original dress, $190.00.
Courtesy McMasters Doll Auctions.

20" hard plastic "Nancy Lee,"
MIB, $450.00.
Courtesy Cathie Clark.

"Nancy,"
MIB, $300.00.
Courtesy Cathie Clark.

Artisan Novelty Company

Artisan Novelty Co. (Gardena, CA, 1950+) made hard plastic Miss Gadabout, Raving Beauty, and other fashion-type dolls with small waists and a suggestion of breasts. They generally featured a "grown-up" wardrobe of evening dresses, bride's dresses, negligees, as well as day dresses and skating costumes.

18" hard plastic, "Raving Beauty" by Artisan Novelty Company, $295.00.
Courtesy Debbie Crume.

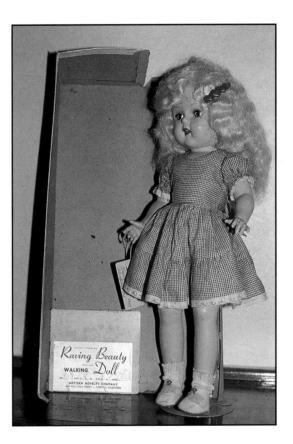

"Raving Beauty" walker by Artisan Novelty Company, 325.00.
Courtesy Cathie Clark.

Artist Dolls

These consist of original, one of a kind, limited edition, or limited production dolls of any medium (cloth, porcelain, wax, wood, vinyl, or other material) made for sale to the public. While a hot debate goes on in some doll-making and collecting circles as to the exact definition of an artist doll, we will use the above definition in this category. Some dolls appear to be works of art and some collectors may wish to have just that in their collection. Others define a doll as a play object and like to collect them for such. You, as a collector, are free to make your own decision to suit yourself. Still we can all appreciate the creativity which these talented artists exhibit.

Left: 18" bisque, "Emma Clear," Parian-type lady, $350.00.

Right: 19" bisque, Parian-type man, $350.00.
Courtesy McMasters Doll Auctions.

**Doll artist Dewees Cochran
and her composition dolls.**
Courtesy Millie Busch.

**Composition, "Kathy"
by Dewees Cochran, $1,850.00.**
Courtesy Millie Busch.

**33" porcelain, "Atlantis" by Susan
Dunham, extensive hand beading,
1993, No price available.**

**Composition, "Amber Ann"
by Dewees Cochran, $2,000.00.**
Courtesy Millie Busch.

27

21" porcelain, Susan Dunham's "Charlotte Rose," one of a kind,
circa 1994, No price available.

Courtesy Rosalie Whyel Museum of Doll Art.

21" porcelain, "Madame Bovary,"
one-of-a-kind, private collection, circa 1992, $10,000.00.
Courtesy Susan Dunham.

Artist Dolls

18" porcelain, "Michelle"
by Susan Dunham, 1995, $1,000.00.

Left: 16" porcelain, "Desdemona" by Susan
Dunham, $500.00.

Right: 17" "Othello" by Susan Dunham,
souvenir doll, circa 1991, $500.00.
Courtesy Susan Dunham.

18" resin and cloth, "The Quilter,"
by June Goodnow, circa 1995, $500.00.

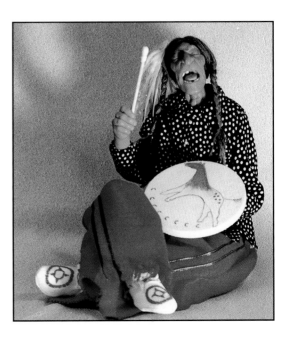

14" one-of-a-kind doll made of Cernit,
$3,000.00.
Courtesy June Goodnow.

6", carved wood, "Hitty Family" by Patti Hale, $300.00 each.
Courtesy Patti Hale.

Two 6" carved wooden "Hitty" dolls by Patti Hale, $300.00 each.
Courtesy Patti Hale.

16" wooden child, hand carved, $650.00.
Courtesy NIADA artist Patti Hale.

Two carved wooden dolls by Pattie Hale, $750.00+ ea.
Courtesy Patti Hale.

10½" characters designed by Mary Moline from Norman Rockwell illustrations, circa 1986, $100.00.
Courtesy Angie Gonzales.

18" porcelain, "Baby," limited edition of 75, $495.00.
Courtesy Linda Lee Sutton Originals.

Elka Hutchen's porcelain, cloth body, "Jack & Jill," mid 1980s, $1,500.00.
Courtesy Tony Winder.

Elka Hutchen's porcelain, "Laura Lee," cloth body, mid 1980s. $1,000.00+.
Courtesy Tony Winder.

21" porcelain, "Bride," limited edition of 10, $825.00.
Courtesy Linda Lee Sutton Originals.

1995 Award of Excellence,
"Chelsea Cherub and Her Heavenly Wardrobe,"
$895.00.
Courtesy Linda Lee Sutton Originals.

Chelsea Cherub &
Her Heavenly Wardrobe
by
Linda Lee Sutton
for Linda Lee Sutton Originals

has received a nomination for a

THE COLLECTOR'S MAGAZINE

DOLLS

1995 AWARD OF EXCELLENCE

*in recognition of its excellence
in conception, design and creation*

Georgene Averill

Georgene Averill (ca. 1915+ New York City, NY) made composition and cloth dolls operating as Madame Georgene Dolls, Averill Mfg. Co., Georgene Novelties, and Madame Hendren. The first line was felt dressed dolls. She made Lyf-Lyk and the Wonder line and patented the Mama Doll in 1918. She designed dolls for Borgfeldt, including Bonnie Babe. Her Peaches was a Patsy-type doll. A very talented doll designer and maker, she made wonderful costumes and cloth and composition dolls. The family had ties to Arranbee, as some in-laws worked in production at that firm. Averill's whistling line of dolls with bellows in the cloth body to allow a whistling sound were clever and were made to portray different occupations or ethnic backgrounds.

13" composition, has cloth body with bellows mechanism, doll makes noise when bounced on feet, painted eyes, open mouth, $300.00.

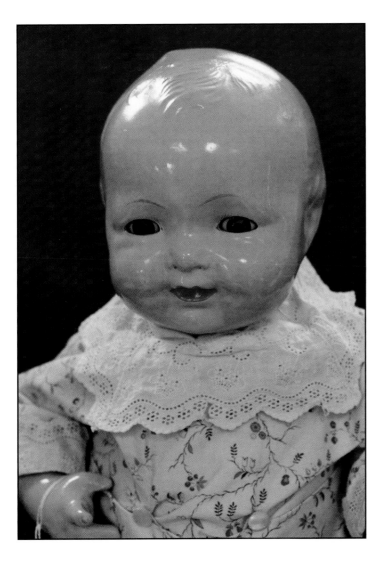

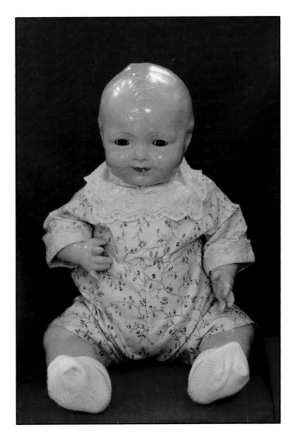

17" baby by Georgene Averill, composition head, arms, and legs, with a cloth body, blue tin sleep eyes, open/closed mouth with one painted tooth, painted molded blond hair, disk jointed, $300.00.
Courtesy Janet Hill.

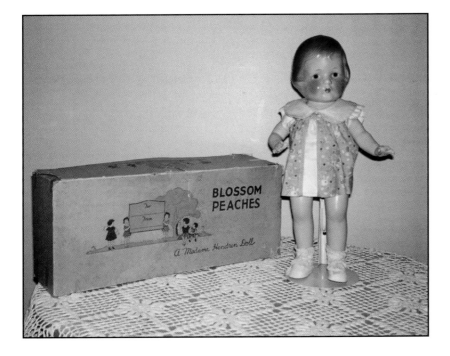

Composition, Georgene Averill "Blossom Peaches," $350.00.
Courtesy June Friel.

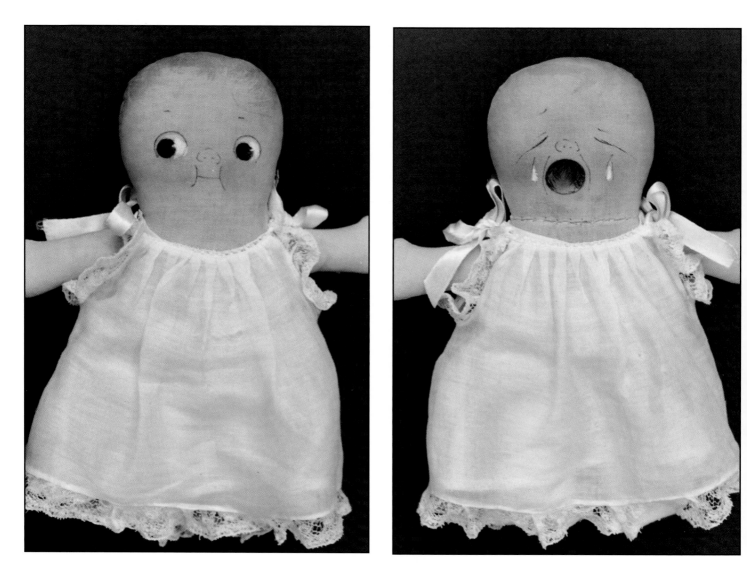

**11" cloth, "Dolly Dingle," "Dottie Dingle," or "Happy Cry,"
painted features, two faced, all original, $450.00.**
Courtesy Sherryl Shirran.

Barbie

Mattel began making Barbie in 1959 in Hawthorne, CA. She remains a top collectible as children have grown up and become avid collectors of their childhood dolls. Of interest to collectors, too, are the fashion trends reflected by Barbie doll's seemingly endless wardrobe.

Marks:

1959–62: BARBIE TM/PATS. PEND.//© MCMLVIII//by//Mattel, Inc.

1963–68: Midge TM© 1962//BARBIE ®/© 1958//BY//Mattel, Inc.

1964–66: © 1958//Mattel, Inc. //U.S. Patented//U.S. Pat. Pend.

1966–69: © 1966//Mattel, Inc.//U.S. Patented//U.S. Pat. Pend//Made in Japan

Description of the first five Barbies:

Number One Barbie Doll, 1959

11½" *heavy* solid vinyl body, *faded white skin color, white irises, pointed eyebrows,* soft brunette or blonde ponytail, black and white striped bathing suit, *holes with metal cylinders in balls of feet* to fit round-pronged stand, gold hoop earrings.

Number Two Barbie Doll, 1959–1960

11½" *heavy* solid vinyl body, faded white skin color, white irises, pointed eyebrows, no holes in feet, some with pearl earrings, soft brunette or blonde ponytail.

Number Three Barbie Doll, 1960

11½" heavy solid vinyl body, *some fading* in skin color, *blue irises, curved eyebrows, no holes in feet,* soft brunette or blonde ponytail.

Number Four Barbie Doll, 1960

11½", same as #3, but solid body of *skin-toned vinyl.*

Number Five Barbie Doll, 1961

11½", vinyl head, now less heavy, *hollow hard plastic body,* firmer texture saran ponytail that now can be red, arm tag.

11½" vinyl, Mattel, #3 Ponytail "Barbie"
doll, all original in box, $550.00.
Courtesy McMaster Doll Auctions.

11½" vinyl, Mattel,
#6 Ponytail "Barbie" doll,
$520.00.
Courtesy McMaster Doll Auctions.

11½" vinyl, #1 "Barbie" doll, be careful easing
the leg joint prior to placing on stand. This
unusual Barbie reportedly came with factory
braid instead of the regular ponytail, $9,000.00.
Courtesy Margie's Doll House.

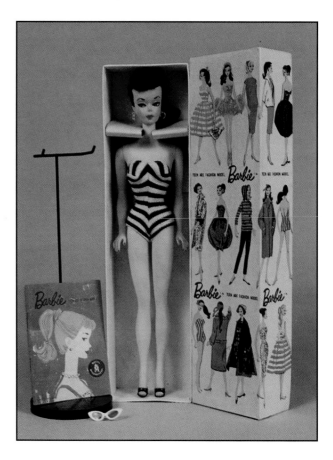

11½" vinyl, Mattel, #2 Ponytail "Barbie" doll,
MIB, $5,100.00.
Courtesy McMasters Doll Auctions.

**11½" #1 "Barbie" doll by Mattel,
with black and white swimsuit, box, stand,
$5,000.00.**
Courtesy Cathie Clark.

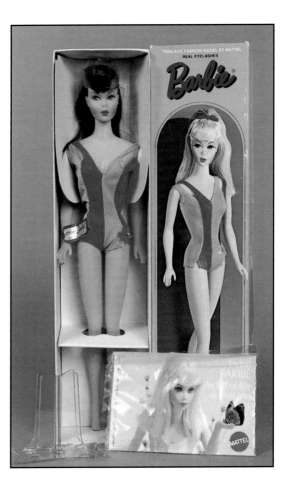

**11½" vinyl, Mattel, standard "Barbie" doll,
brunette, circa 1967, MIB, $625.00.**
Courtesy McMasters Doll Auctions.

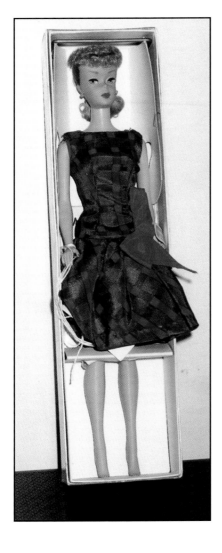

**#4 "Barbie" doll, box, in Beau Time outfit,
$225.00.**
Courtesy Sally McVey.

**11½" "Fashion Photo Barbie," with all accessories,
$100.00+.**
Courtesy Cathie Clark.

11½" vinyl, Mattel, "Skipper" doll, $275.00.
Courtesy McMasters Doll Auctions.

Betsy McCall

Betsy McCall was a paper doll carried in the *McCall's* magazine for many years. About 1952–53, Ideal had Bernard Lipfert design a doll after the paper doll. This 14" Betsy McCall doll had a vinyl head, used a P marked Toni body, and had a glued on saran wig. She was marked "McCall Corp." on the head, and "Ideal Doll//P-90" on her back. She came with a McCall pattern for making an apron. In about 1958, American Character made an 8" hard plastic Betsy McCall, and circa 1959 a 35" Betsy McCall with vinyl head and limbs and a plastic body.

**"Betsy McCall," child fashion doll,
as seen in *McCall's* magazine, $175.00.**
Courtesy Cathie Clark.

Betsy McCall

8" hard plastic, with jointed knees, seven extra outfits in trunk, circa 1958, $265.00.
Courtesy Sally McVey.

20" vinyl, "Betsy McCall," $300.00.
Courtesy Shirley Grime.

38" "Sonny McCall," $725.00, and 36" "Betsy McCall," $625.00.
Courtesy Iva Mae Jones.

Cameo Doll Company

Joseph L. Kallus's company operated from 1922 to 1930+, in New York City, and Port Allegheny, Pa. They made composition dolls with segmented wooden or cloth bodies.

**19" composition, "Baby Blossom," composition upper torso, arms,
and head, cloth lower body and legs, molded hair,
green tin sleep eyes, open mouth, teeth, all original,
marked "DES & Copyright//by J.L. Kallus//Made in U.S.A,"
$1,000.00.**
Courtesy Janet Hill.

Cameo Doll Company

**12" composition
"Giggles," boxed, $350.00.**
Courtesy McMasters Doll Auctions.

**11" composition
"Betty Boop," $475.00.**
Courtesy McMasters Doll Auctions.

Composition, "Joy Doll," $300.00.
Courtesy Sherryl Shirran.

**Composition "Joy" dolls designed by Joseph
Kallus, circa 1932, 10" $275.00,
and 15" $450.00.** *Courtesy Joy M. Kramer.*

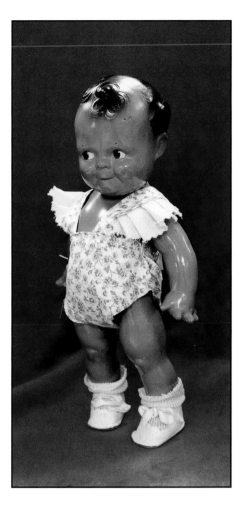

14" composition "Scootles," designed by Rose O' Neill,
original romper suit, dimples, smiling mouth,
circa 1925, $475.00.
Courtesy Stephanie Prince.

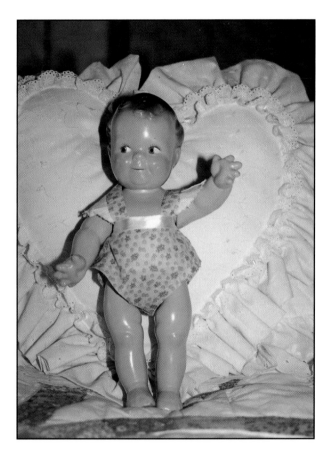

Composition "Scootles," $400.00.
Courtesy Pat Schuda.

**15" composition "Scootles," restored
by Oleta Woodside, $350.00.**
Courtesy Marian Pettygrove.

Composition

Cold press composition, used around 1890, describes the method of putting a mixture of ingredients (composition) into molds. The recipe for composition varied with each manufacturer. At first glue was used to bind together such things as flour, shredded cardboard or paper, rags, and then later sawdust and wood pulp as manufacturers learned how to bake the composition in multiple molds in the hot press method. The mixture contained more liquid when poured into molds than when pressed and the ingredients differed somewhat.

These doll heads were first described as indestructible when compared to the bisque and china heads that could be easily broken. The dolls were dipped in tinted glue baths to give a flesh tone and then later the features and coloring was air brushed. Humidity made it difficult for the dolls to dry correctly in early production procedures, but later techniques were refined to reduce this problem. The big problem with composition dolls was their glycerin and glue base — when the surface became saturated with water, it would disintegrate. Extremes of heat and humidity cause bacteria to grow on the surface and destroy the painted finish.

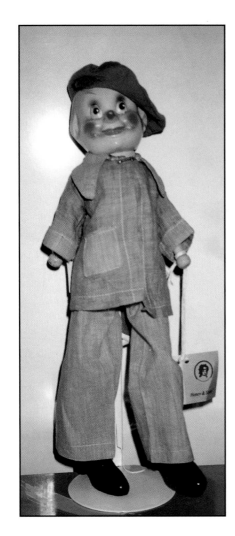

Collectors need to keep composition dolls away from direct sunlight, avoid extremes of temperature, and keep a gauge in their cases to check the relative humidity. When the relative humidity exceeds 85%, bacteria have opportune conditions to grow and destroy the painted surfaces. Composition dolls should not be stored in plastic, but wrapped in cotton fabric that has been washed and well rinsed to remove any soap or conditioner that may be present. Collectors who had this type of doll as a plaything in their childhood can, with a little caution, enjoy some of the wide variety of dolls still available.

16½" composition and wood character "Pinocchio" doll, $425.00.
Courtesy Sharon Kolibaba.

14" composition head, plush body,
compo boots, unknown maker,
$350.00.
Courtesy Sherryl Shirran.

Marked "Portuguese" on foot, this was an entrant
to a late 1930's World Fair, $275.00.
Courtesy Debbie Crume.

Composition, Dutch pair, $175.00 ea.
Courtesy Dee Domroe.

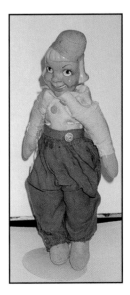

Thought to be advertising doll for
Dutch Boy Paint, $225.00.
Courtesy Debbie Crume.

Composition Dolls

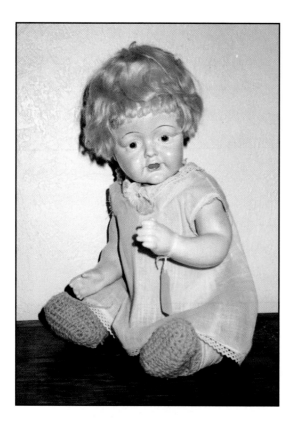

**All composition doll,
marked "DECO" on back of neck,
painted eyes, mohair wig, $325.00.**
Courtesy Betty Haddix.

**12" composition,
Fleischaker Novelty Company "Beverly Doll,"
$275.00.**
Courtesy Dee Cermak.

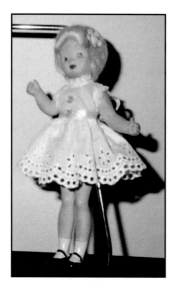

**Composition, Margit Nilsen's
"Thumbls Up Doll," $75.00.**
Courtesy Millie Busch.

**10" composition,
"Maiden America," $125.00.**
Courtesy Millie Busch.

19" composition, "Child,"
with painted hair, all original, $300.00.
Courtesy Connie Lee Martin.

Doll with hoop in dotted dress, composition type
head, painted features, stuffed cloth body with
armature, tag reads "Old//Cottage//Toys//Had
Made in Great Britain," $125.00.
Courtesy Peggy Millhouse.

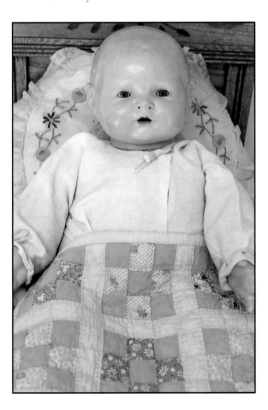

18" composition, "Hush-A-Bye-Babe,"
composition head and hands, cloth body,
printed on body "Hush-A-Bye/Babe/Pat. Appl'd
for/The Doll that Breathes," all original, $450.00.
Courtesy Sherryl Shirran.

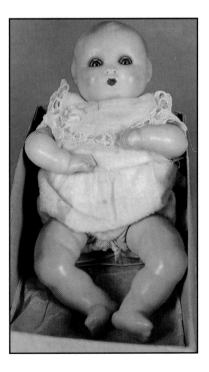

8" composition, German "Puz," baby
original white shirt, box, $220.00.
Courtesy McMasters Doll Auctions.

Composition dressmaking doll with McCall
patterns, jointed arms, painted molded hair,
$125.00.
Courtesy Cathie Clark.

"Thumb's Up Doll," tag reads "Your purchase of
this doll helps in sending Ambulances to Britain
and her Allies and Vitamins to the undernourished
children of England. An original creation of Margit
Nilsen Studios, Inc.," $125.00.
Courtesy Bev Mitchell.

27" all composition, "Peggy,"
Paris Doll Company, walking legs,
unmarked, circa 1940, $425.00.
Courtesy Sherryl Shirran.

8" composition, "Thumb's Up," tag reads "The manufacturer
of this official Thumbs Up Doll is participating in the Buy To
Aid Britain Campaign by donating a portion of his profit on
this sale to Ambulances to Britain," $125.00.
Courtesy Bev Mitchell.

Cosmopolitan

Cosmopolitan made an 8" hard plastic doll to compete with Vogue's Ginny during the 1950s. They also made high heel dolls in about 1957, and used a Little Miss Ginger chorus line in their TV ad campaign to promote their dolls.

8" vinyl, "Little Miss Ginger," slim doll with high heels, MIB, $150.00.
Courtesy Cathie Clark.

Ginger's teen-age sister, "Miss Ginger," a high heel vinyl fashion-type doll, $160.00.
Courtesy Cathie Clark.

10½" vinyl "Miss Ginger," with high heeled feet, extra wardrobe, 1957, $160.00.
Courtesy Cathie Clark.

10½" vinyl, "Miss Ginger," $160.00.
Courtesy Cathie Clark.

Deluxe Reading

Deluxe Reading manufactured dolls from 1957 to 1965 that were sold at supermarkets as premiums — a reward for purchasing something else or for totaling a certain figure. They were marketed with several names: Deluxe Premium Corp., Deluxe Reading, Deluxe Topper, Deluxe Toy Creations, Topper Corp., and Topper Toys. They were of stuffed vinyl, jointed at the neck only, with sleep eyes and rooted hair. The dolls were inexpensively dressed as brides or in long formals. They also made 8" vinyl Penny Brite dolls with side-glancing eyes and a vinyl carrying case.

6½" all vinyl, Topper Corporation, "Dawn," jointed, rooted hair, posable, with extra wardrobe and friends, 1970 – 1971, $45.00.
Courtesy Cathie Clark.

Deluxe Reading

High heel fashion-type doll, with wardrobe,
$85.00.
Courtesy Cathie Clark.

Vinyl "Little Miss Fashion Doll," included four outfits in her wardrobe, circa 1957, $125.00.
Courtesy Cathie Clark.

24" stuffed vinyl, jointed only at neck, sleep eyes,
rooted hair, earrings, original pink formal,
grocery store premium, $85.00.
Private Collection

Effanbee

Bernard Fleishaker and Hugo Baum formed a partnership, Fleischaker and Baum, in 1910 in New York City that would eventually be known as Effanbee. They began making rag and crude composition dolls and even had Lenox make some bisque heads for them. They developed a very high quality composition doll with a high quality finish. This characterized their dolls of the 20s and 30s and lasted until after World War II, when the company was sold to Noma Electric. The company declined with the death of Hugo Baum in 1940, but had remarkable success with a series of dolls, including Bubbles, Grumpy, Lovums, Patsy, and Dy-Dee. Effanbee was a very entrepreneurial company during its prominent years using the talents of free-lance doll artist, Bernard Lipfert who created Bubbles, Patsy, and Dy-Dee as well as Shirley Temple for Ideal, the Dionne Quintuplets for Alexander, and Ginny for Vogue.

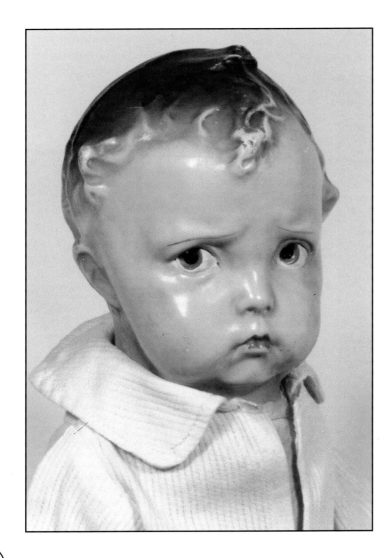

14" composition head, "Baby Grumpy," heavily molded hair, intaglio painted eyes, frowning brows, closed mouth, cloth body, $350.00.
Private Collection

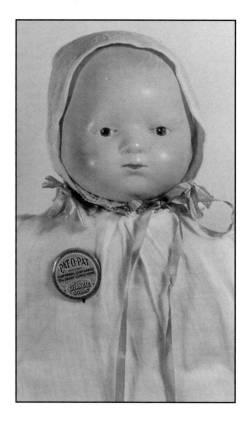

Pair of "Grumpykins" dressed in Pennsylvania Dutch costumes as Dunkards,
$400.00 for pair.
Private Collection

14" composition "Pat-O-Pat," newborn baby
with cloth body containing
mechanism that when squeezed allows hands to
clap, wears original outfit, pinback button,
$350.00.

Composition "Little Lady Bride," mohair wig,
sleep eyes, all original, $375.00.
Courtesy Oleta Woodside.

Composition "Little Ladys," in negligee and matching
undies, mohair wigs, sleep eyes, closed mouths, $325.00+.
Courtesy Oleta Woodside.

20½" "Little Lady,"
in taffeta evening dress, $300.00.
Courtesy Ann Van Arnum.

27" "Little Lady," with gold heart hand-tag,
all original in velveteen dress and bolero, human
hair wig, blue sleep eyes, $500.00+.
Courtesy Vickie Applegate.

Composition "Harmonica Joe," original
clothes, bluebird pin, $350.00.
Courtesy Chad Moyer.

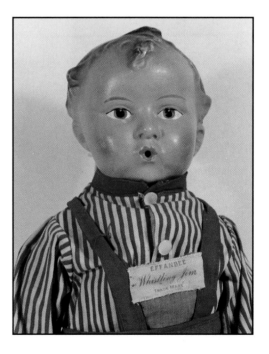

Composition "Whistling Jim," original
tagged clothes, molded hair, painted eyes,
open mouth, bellows mechanism in body
allows Jim to whistle, $350.00.
Courtesy Chad Moyer.

Effanbee

25" composition "Rosemary," human hair wig, blue tin eyes, original chain necklace, circa 1925, $435.00.
Private Collection

18" composition "Cliquot Eskimo," with felt hands, cloth body, mohair suit and hat, circa 1920s, $500.00.
Courtesy Sherryl Shirran.

15" vinyl, Jan Hagara "Cristina," lst limited edition doll with signed tag, circa 1983, $200.00.
Courtesy Angie Gonzales.

19" hard plastic "Honey Walker," boxed, $425.00.
Courtesy McMasters Doll Auctions.

18" hard plastic "Honey Bride,"
tag reads "I am Junior Miss," $295.00.
Courtesy Margie Welker.

15" composition American Children
Series "Barbara Joan," $600.00.
Courtesy Jan Drugan.

17" composition "Little Lady,"
with trunk and wardrobe, $500.00.
Courtesy Barb Comienski.

21" composition, "Honey," $350.00.
Courtesy Margie Welker.

Composition "Sugar Pie,"
with wrist tag, all original, $400.00.
Courtesy Candy McCain.

21" composition "Little Lady,"
near mint, $350.00.
Courtesy Martha Sweeney.

18" composition "Little Lady Bride,"
all original, hair piece added, $275.00.
Courtesy Jacquie Duran.

21" composition "Little Lady," all original, $275.00.
Courtesy Sue Wilkins.

**Composition "Little Lady Bride,"
$300.00.**
Courtesy Pat Schuda.

**14" composition
"Historical 1939," all original, $550.00.**
Courtesy Bev Mitchell.

14" composition "Suzanne," $265.00.
Courtesy Dorothy Vaughn.

**18" composition "Lovums Toddler,"
original dress and bonnet, $350.00.**
Courtesy Marilyn Ramsey.

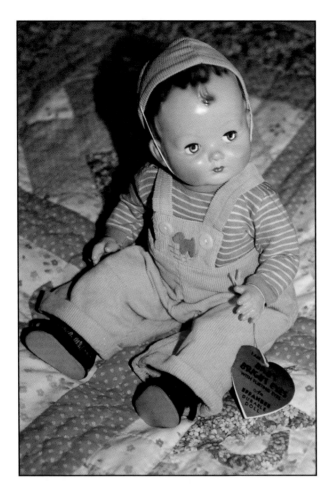

**Composition
"Baby Bright Eyes," $350.00.**
Courtesy Pat Schuda.

Close-up showing original hang-tag from above.

**Composition "Little Lady," in box, yarn hair,
fancy long evening dress with fur cape,
embroidered inside "Little Lady," $600.00.**
Courtesy Amanda Hash.

**Composition "Gaye,"
Little Lady, $400.00.**
Courtesy Jan Drugan.

**Composition "Suzanne," with trunk and
wardrobe, circa 1940, $500.00.**
Courtesy Sylvia Kleindinst.

**15" composition "Coquette,"
unmarked, all original, circa 1912,
$400.00.**
Courtesy Sherryl Shirran.

THE PATSY FAMILY

Another one of Effanbee's great success stories was the Patsy doll designed by Bernard Lipfert and advertised in 1928. She almost was not named Patsy. The same doll was advertised as Mimi in 1927 and Patsy in 1928. Patsy was one of the first dolls to have a wardrobe manufactured just for her. Accessories and clothing were sold not only by Effanbee but other manufacturers as well. She was made of all composition and her patent was hotly defended by Effanbee. What was actually patented was a neck joint that allowed the doll to pose and stand alone. She portrayed a 3-year-old girl with short bobbed red hair and a molded headband, painted side-glancing eyes, pouty mouth, and bent right arm. She wore simple classic dresses closed with a safety pin. She had a golden heart charm bracelet and/or a gold paper heart tag with her name.

Patsy was so popular she soon had several sisters, many variations, and even a boy friend, Skippy. Effanbee promoted Patsy sales with a newspaper *The Patsytown News* that went to a reported quarter million children. Effanbee also had an Aunt Patsy that toured the country promoting their dolls. In addition, they formed a Patsy Doll Club and gave free pinback membership buttons to children who wrote in or bought a Patsy doll. Effanbee tied their doll line to popular current events such as producing George and Martha Washington for the bicentennial of George's birth. They costumed a group of dolls like the White Horse Inn Operetta that toured the U.S. During the war years, they fashioned military uniforms for the Skippy dolls and also costumed dolls in ethnic dress (Dutch) or after characters in books like *Alice In Wonderland*.

The death of Hugo Baum in 1940 and the loss of income during the war years threw Effanbee into decline. In 1946, Effanbee was sold to Noma Electric. They reissued a 1946 Patsy and later a new 17" Patsy Joan. Since that time, the company changed hands several more times, until it was bought by Stanley and Irene Wahlberg, the present owners. Limited editions of Patsy Ann and Skippy were issued during the 1970s, and Patsy reappeared in vinyl in the 1980s. The Wahlbergs reissued Patsy Joan in 1995. In 1996 and 1997 they will issue a new group of Patsy, Skippy, and Wee Patsy dolls in vinyl painted to look like the old composition ones. These are already becoming collectibles.

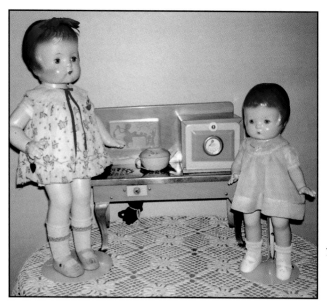

19" composition "Patsy Ann," $350.00, and 13½" "Patsy," $325.00, shown with old metal electric stove.
Courtesy June Friel.

**Black "Patsy Joan,"
with black wig, 1946, $650.00+.**
Courtesy Trish Sheppard.

**Left: Current reissue of 1946 "Patsy Joan"
in Alice in Wonderland dress, $150.00.**

**Right: F.A.O. Schwarz special dressed in
replica of 1934 outfit, $225.00.**
Courtesy Millie Busch.

**11½" "Patricia-kin" in pink flocked dress,
with matching hat, circa 1939, $450.00.**
Courtesy Pat Schuda.

**15" "Patricia" as Martha Washington,
in fancy dress, replaced lace and bows,
white mohair wig, circa 1935+,
$400.00.**
Courtesy Pat Schuda.

Effanbee

9½" "Patsyette Wedding Party," five dolls, all original outfits, dressed as bride, groom, minister, best man, and bridesmaid, $1,250.00+ set.
Courtesy Ann Tuma.

Composition "Patsyette," all original, $325.00. *Courtesy Mary Lee Swope.*

Composition "Patsy Baby Huggers," cloth body, snaps on hand allow dolls to snap together to dance or hug, $500.00 pair.
Courtesy Margaret Long.

Composition "Patsyette," with wig, in The White Horse Inn costume, inspired by White Horse Inn musical stage play brought over from Europe, $500.00+.
Courtesy Elizabeth Dorsey.

16" all composition "Patsy Joan," with bracelet and paper hang-tag, in tagged aqua pique dress with yellow trim and matching hat with ties, $500.00.
Courtesy Bev Mitchell.

19" composition "Patsy-Ann" boxed, $500.00.
Courtesy McMasters Doll Auctions.

14" composition "Skippy," boxed, $725.00.
Courtesy McMasters Doll Auctions.

10" composition "Patsy Baby," $325.00.
Courtesy Marie R. Gardyne.

Effanbee

Composition "Patsy Mae,"
$1,200.00+.
Courtesy Barbara DeFeo.

Two 8" composition
"Baby Tinyettes," $275.00 ea.
Courtesy Barbara DeFeo.

11½" composition
"Patricia-Kin," $350.00.
Courtesy Lucia Kirsch.

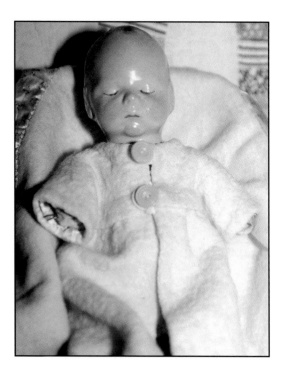

Composition "Babyette," $250.00.
Courtesy Cherie Gervais.

11½" composition
"Patsykin" (Patsy Jr.), with trunk and
wardrobe, $500.00.
Courtesy Teri Pierce.

13½" composition "Patsy,"
Glad Togs outfit, $425.00.
Courtesy Virginia Vinton.

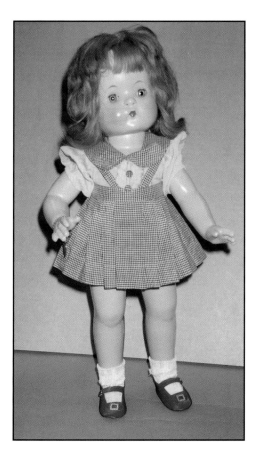

19" composition
"Patsy Ann," $500.00.
Courtesy Bev Mitchell.

6" composition "Fairy Princess"
(Wee Patsy) with Fairy Castle Dollhouse box,
$475.00. *Courtesy Pat Schuda.*

Effanbee

13½" composition "Patsy,"
in copy of 1930s bridal dress by
Barbara Schletzbaum, $400.00.
Courtesy Marilyn Ramsey.

6" composition "Wee Patsy"
as Collen Moore Fairy Princess, $350.00.
Courtesy Sue Wilkins.

Two 19" composition
"Patsy Ann" dolls, $400.00 ea.
Courtesy Marian Pettygrove.

Four 9½" composition "Patsyette" dolls,
$350.00 – 400.00.
Courtesy Pat Schuda.

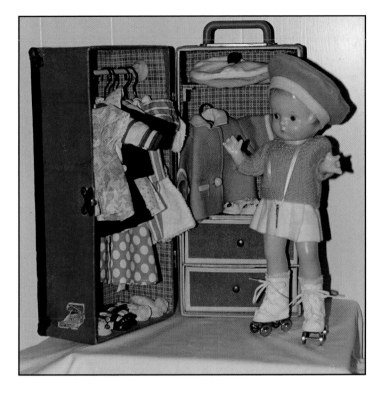

11½" composition "Patsy-Kins" (Patsy Jr.),
with trunk and wardrobe, $500.00+.
Courtesy Marian Pettygrove.

11½" composition "Patsy-Kins" (Patsy Jr.),
wearing felt coat and hat, $400.00.
Courtesy Marian Pettygrove.

11½" composition "Patsy Joan,"
in original green print dress, $450.00.
Courtesy Marian Pettygrove.

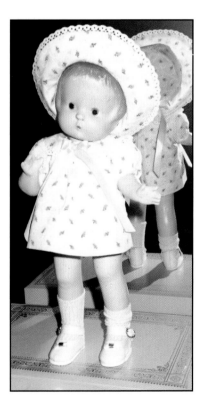

14" composition "Patsy,"
$350.00.
Courtesy Mildred L. Carol.

19" composition "Patsy," re-dressed in
red hat and romper suit, $325.00.
Courtesy Mildred L. Carol.

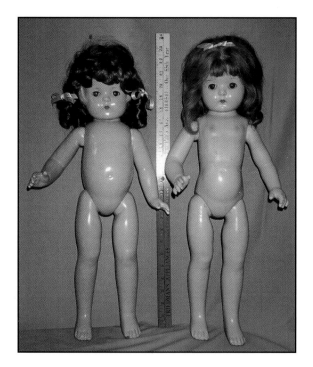

Left: 22" "Patsy Lou," $575.00.

Right: 24" "Patricia Lou."
Both composition, both nude, $600.00.
(Prices are for dolls dressed in original outfits.)
Courtesy Lorrie A. Wade.

Composition 19" "Patsy Ann," $450.00.
7¾" "Tinyette," $275.00.
Courtesy Diane Gulomo.

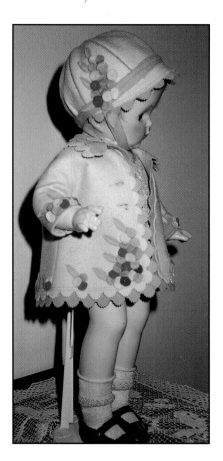

19" composition
"Patsy Ann," in coat, $500.00.
Courtesy Diane Gulomo.

Composition "Today's Girl," all original outfit, was also advertised as "Patricia," cloth body, war-time shortages brought about the use of yarn for hair, cloth for body construction, $350.00.
Courtesy Candy McCain.

Two 19" composition "Patsy Ann" dolls in felt coats, $500.00+ ea. Felt coats like these were produced commercially in a range of sizes to fit Patsy family dolls.
Courtesy Virginia Vinton.

Left: 16" composition "Patsy Joan," in red/white dress, $400.00.

Right: 11½" composition "Patsy Jr.," in pink dress, $350.00.
Courtesy Betty Fronefield.

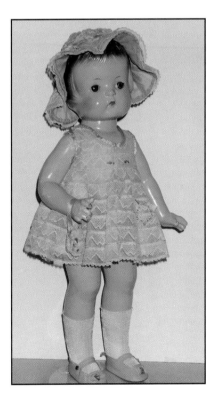

22" composition "Patsy Lou," $525.00.
Courtesy Betty Fronefield.

Effanbee

Two 19" composition
"Patsy Ann" dolls $550.00 ea.
Courtesy Betty Fronefield.

14" composition "Patsy," variant with Patsy
Baby head on Patsy body, in original box
with hang-tag, $650.00.
Courtesy Eleanor Selmer.

17" composition "Patsy Joan,"
all original, tagged dress, $450.00.
Courtesy Pat Smith.

17" composition "Patsy Joan," all
original in white dot dress with bonnet, $425.00.
Courtesy Pat Smith.

Two 15" composition "Twin Patricia" dolls both
dressed alike, left with red trim, $500.00, right with
blue trim, $750.00, with trunk and wardrobe.
Courtesy Pat Smith.

16" composition "Patsy Joan," all original
with hang-tag, circa 1946, $500.00.
Courtesy Pat Smith.

Two 9½" composition "George and Martha
Washington Patsyette" dolls, $425.00 ea.
Courtesy Jan Drugan.

18" composition "Betty Bounce," with
Patsy Ann body and Lovums head,
$350.00.
Private Collection.

Effanbee

9½" composition,
"Patsy Tinyette," $350.00.
Courtesy Jan Drugan.

16" composition "Patsy Joan,"
in green dress with bonnet, $475.00.
Courtesy Jan Drugan.

25 – 26" composition "Patsy Ruth,"
all original, $1,100.00.
Courtesy Victoria Applegate.

10 – 11" composition "Patsy Baby Twins,"
dressed alike in basket, $750.00.
Courtesy Victoria Applegate.

9½" composition "Patsyette,"
in green dress, $350.00.
Courtesy Jan Drugan.

9" composition "Patsy Babyette," all original
in white outfit, with blue tin sleep eyes,
$325.00.
Private Collection.

17" composition "Patsy Joan," in blue and white
dress with bonnet, circa 1946, $400.00.
16" "Patsy Joan," in Glad Togs beach pajamas
and matching hat, circa 1931, $500.00.
Courtesy Marilyn Ramsey.

16" composition "Patsy Joan," in blue
coat and hat, circa 1931, $425.00.
Courtesy Marilyn Ramsey.

9½" composition "Patsyette,"
with trunk and wardrobe, $600.00.
Courtesy Betty Fronefield.

9" composition "Patsyette,"
all original in her red wardrobe box,
$750.00.
Courtesy Mary Lee Stallings.

16" composition "Patsy Joan," in
original costume inspired by White
Horse Inn musical, $750.00.
Courtesy Marilyn Ramsey.

14" composition "Patsy,"
$475.00.
Courtesy Betty Fronefield.

14" composition "Patsy,"
in original swim suit and cap,
tagged "Kute Togs," $500.00.
Courtesy Shirlijeanne of Kandyland Dolls.

DY-DEE

The "Almost Human Doll"

Effanbee contracted with Marie Whitman who had developed a drink/wet valve mechanism that would allow a doll to "drink" and then "wet." Effanbee used the talents of Bernard Lipfert to sculpt a doll head with molded ears that was to be made of hard rubber. They contracted the bodies out to Miller Rubber Co. of Akron, OH. The idea of a doll wetting its diaper was considered in poor taste and the doll was rejected by Harrods in London, until one of the royal family requested one.

The doll was referred to as the "Almost Human Doll" in promotions. Dy-Dee Baby was introduced in April of 1934, in two sizes. It was available with layettes and trunks or all were sold separately. By 1935, Dy-Dees came in several sizes, 11" Dy-Dee-Ette, 13" Dy-Dee-Kin , 15" Dy-Dee, and 20" Dy-Dee Ann, that soon became Dy-Dee Lou. Aunt Patsy was the official spokesperson on Dy-Dee care.

In 1936, there was a new Golden Treasure Chest to hold Dy-Dee's wardrobe as well as a bathinette to bathe her and a buggy to carry her places. An instruction booklet was now included with Dy-Dee entitled, "What Every Young Doll Mother Should Know."

The book *Dy-Dee Doll's Days* was featured in Dy-Dee sets in the 1937 Ward's catalog. New accessories included a diaper bag and mother outfit which included a rubber apron, white uniform cap and apron, bath accessories, hot water bottle, and diary.

In 1938, Dy-Dee could blow bubbles with her bubble-pipe and sip from her spoon. A new size was the 9" Dy-Dee-Wee. Queen Holden drew Dy-Dee Baby paper dolls that were published by Whitman. In 1939, advertising showed pink and blue name print pajamas with the Dy-Dee sets.

In 1940, Dy-Dee was revamped to include applied rubbers, real nostrils with holes, and cotton swabs to clean the ears and nose. Now there are three sizes of Dy-Dees, 11", 15", and 20".

In 1941 the 20" Dy-Dee Lou's name was changed to Dy-Dee Louise and Dy-Dee Jane was the 15" doll and Dy-Dee Ellen was 11". New too, were blankets with the Dy-Dee name print. The tousle head caracul wig was new this year as well as striped pajamas. During the war years Dy-Dee was featured with layettes and bathinettes. As the war progressed and rubber shortages appeared, only accessories were promoted — not the dolls.

In 1946, Effanbee was sold to Noma Electric and they began offering Dy-Dee in a travel-type case with handle and lock. Also new was bubble bath in the layette. In 1948, a crier/pacifier was included in the layette and after 1948 tear ducts were added. Dy-Dee was produced in hard plastic and vinyl in the 50s.

15" hard rubber "Dy-Dee Baby," with molded
ears, in original silk coat, hat, and nightgown,
$275.00+.
Courtesy Vickie Applegate.

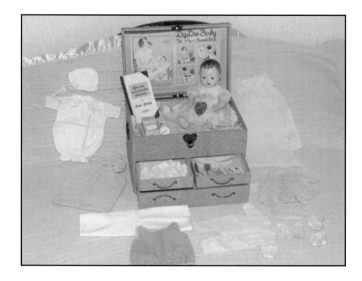

11" Dy-Dee wardrobe box, pieces of original
wardrobe and accessories, $300.00.
Courtesy Peggy Montei.

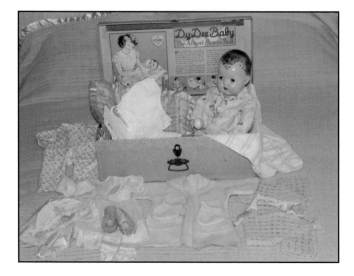

20" "Dy-Dee Lou," with original shoes, robe,
slippers, sweaters, and sleepers, $450.00.
Courtesy Peggy Montei.

20" "Dy-Dee Lou," $450.00, in pink print dress
shown with a 15" "Dy-Dee," in box with her
same print dress still attached to box, $500.00.
Courtesy Peggy Montei.

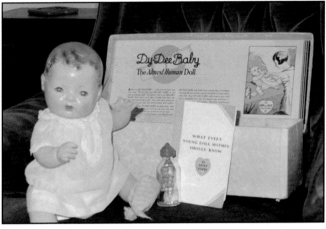

Rubber "Dy-Dee Baby," boxed, $400.00.
Courtesy Louise M. Lunde.

13" "Dy-Dee," with original bunting, print sleepers, and other well-made garments, $250.00.
Courtesy Peggy Montei.

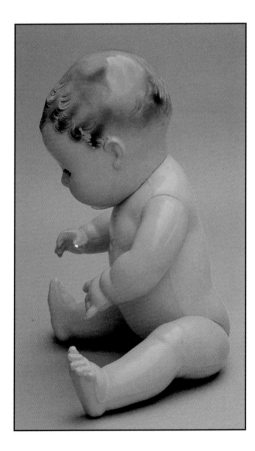

15" hard rubber "Dy-Dee Baby," with molded ears, nude to show rubber body construction, molded painted hair, $200.00.
Courtesy Vickie Applegate.

Vinyl "Dy-Dee Darlyn," $65.00.
Courtesy Barbara Cresenze.

Effanbee

**12" hard rubber Effanbee,
"Dy-Dee Ellen," $175.00.**
Courtesy Iva Mae Jones.

Rubber "Dy-Dee Ellen," $150.00.
Courtesy Pat Schuda.

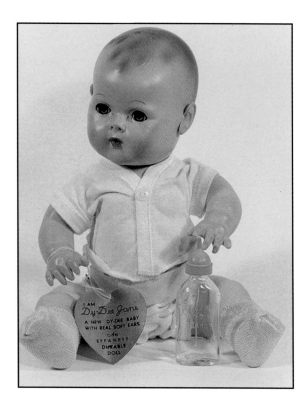

**15" "Dy-Dee Jane," with applied ears,
in diaper, shirt, and socks with
accessories, mint, $275.00.**
Courtesy Angie Gonzales.

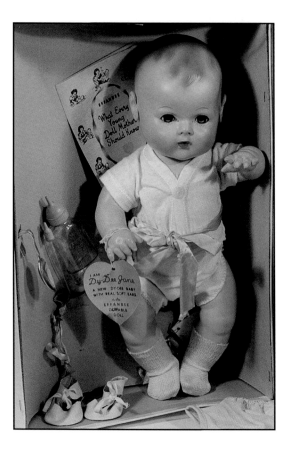

**15" "Dy-Dee Jane," with applied ears,
with accessories, MIB, $375.00.**
Courtesy Angie Gonzales.

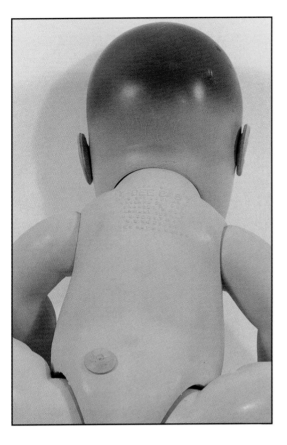

15" "Dy-Dee Jane,"
drink wet outlet on rear lower torso,
marked "Dy-Dee Baby" on her back,
$275.00.
Courtesy Angie Gonzales.

20" hard rubber "Dy-Dee Lou," in original
dress with gold paper hang-tag, $450.00.
Courtesy Angie Gonzales.

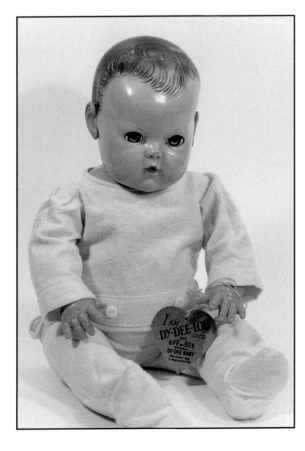

20" hard rubber "Dy-Dee Lou," in original flannel sleeper
with gold paper hang-tag, $425.00. *Courtesy Angie Gonzales.*

20" hard rubber "Dy-Dee Lou," in original
flannel sleeper with gold paper hang-tag,
$425.00. *Courtesy Angie Gonzales.*

Ethnic Dolls

Dolls in national costumes were made of many mediums, including bisque, cloth, composition, hard plastic, and vinyl. During the 30s, 40s, and 50s and later, many dolls dressed in regional costumes could be purchased cheaply as souvenirs in different areas. A wide variety of these dolls are unmarked or made by little known companies.

5 – 13" composition "Jeannine from Alsace-Lorraine," "Colleen of Ireland," "Sophie of Poland," "Katrika of Holland," #5 has no name, $100.00 ea.
Courtesy Patsy Corrigan.

17½" and 15½" vinyl dolls made in Poland, dressed in regional costumes, $70.00 pair.
Courtesy Hank Collins.

10½" rayon stockinette doll in regional costume, from the Soviet Union, $100.00.
Courtesy Amanda Hash.

23" cloth, one-of-a-kind "Ceremonial Dancer," Zuni Pueblo, made by unknown Native American, $65.00.
Private Collection.

Hard plastic ethnic doll with cloth body, synthetic wig, sleep eyes, closed mouth, in regional costume, $30.00.
Courtesy Angie Gonzales.

Girl Scout Dolls

Pidd Miller of Houston, TX, has been instrumental in promoting doll collecting for Girl Scouts and has helped the San Jacinto Girl Scout Council establish a Girl Scout doll collecting patch in 1989. The patch may be earned by any Girl Scout – Daisy to Senior. Pidd Miller has researched scouting and has provided the following information on the Scout movement.

Girl Scouts began in the United States in 1912 for ten- to-seventeen-year old girls and Brownie Scouts began in 1926 for seven- to-nine-year-old girls. The Brownie name was bestowed by Englishman Robert Baden-Powell, who started the Boy and Girl Scouts. He derived the name "Brownie" from an English tale of little people, "brownies" who helped with chores when the family was asleep.

The first Brownie uniform was a tan one-piece dress, with two breast pockets, with or without matching bloomers showing. The peaked cap was of the same material. A recent article in *Newsweek* revealed there had been 175 modifications to the uniform since 1912.

The Girls Scout camp uniform is pictured in the 1920 Girl Scout Hand Book. The uniform is gray-green with a shirt and bloomers below the knee. The tie is red. The socks are green with darker green turned down on top. Her shoes are black with a small heel and they tie at the ankle.

In 1985 the Brownie uniform changed from an A-line jumper to a jumper with a two button big top. A short sleeved blouse has the Brownie emblem and brown stripes with an orange tie.

For more information on the Girl Scout doll collection patch, send a SASE to: *Pidd Miller*
PO Box 631092
Houston, TX 77263

13" all cloth, "75th Anniversary Girl Scout," in copy of early 1900s uniform, circa 1987, $50.00.
Courtesy Angie Gonzales.

8½" vinyl, Effanbee, "Fluffy Brownie Scout,"
and "Blue Bird," all original, marked on head,
1965, $50.00.
Courtesy Angie Gonzales.

12" cloth "Girl Scout," by Angela Bannon,
"Aussie Adventurer" made in Australia, $55.00.
Courtesy Pidd Miller.

16" all cloth, Averill Manufacturing Corporation,
"Girl Scout," $400.00.
Courtesy Diane Miller.

Vinyl, Effanbee, 15" "Patsy Ann Girl Scout," $350.00; 14" "Suzette Brownie," $325.00;
11½" "Fluffy Cadette," $300.00; 8" black "Fluffy Junior," $200.00; 11½" "Brownie, $75.00;
8" "Pumpkin Junior," $50.00; and 11" "Brownie," $75.00.
Courtesy Diane Miller.

15" vinyl, Effanbee,
"Patsy Ann Girl Scout," $350.00,
and "Suzette Brownie," $325.00.
Courtesy Diane Miller.

11" vinyl, Effanbee, "Brownie Scout," $75.00.
Courtesy Marjory Collins.

8" vinyl, Madame Alexander, unofficial "Girl Scout," $60.00.
Courtesy Diane Miller.

5" cloth, Girl Scout "Teddy Bear," $35.00.
Courtesy Marjory Collins.

Vinyl, Uneeda "Girl Scout," and "Brownie," boxed, $150.00 ea.
Courtesy Diane Miller.

Hard plastic "Girl Scouts," dressed by Terri Lee, two 16", $50.00 ea.; two 10", $225.00 ea.; two 8", $200.00.
Courtesy Diane Miller.

Girl Scout Dolls

10" cloth, Norah Wellings "Girl Guide from England," circa 1943, $125.00.
Courtesy Diane Miller.

All cloth, Georgene Averill "Brownie," $250.00.
Courtesy Diane Miller.

13½" all cloth, Georgene Averill "Brownie," and "Girl Scout," $250.00 ea.
Courtesy Diane Miller.

Vinyl "Patsy Ann," $300.00; "Fluffy," $175.00; "Katie," $75.00; and "Wendy" dolls by Effanbee, Cameo, and Madame Alexander, $60.00.
Courtesy Georgia Henry.

Vinyl, modern Effanbee,
"Brownie & Girl Scout,"
$125.00 ea.
Courtesy Angie Gonzales.

**All cloth artist doll,
"Girl Scout Brownie," $75.00.**
Courtesy Georgia Henry.

**17" composition, Effanbee "Patsy Joan,"
with beautiful coloring in original
Girl Scout uniform, $600.00.**
Courtesy Lilian K. Booth.

Hard Plastic

Plastics came into use during World War II. The war and shortages of some materials caused great upheavals in the toy industry as some plants had been converted to make items for the war effort. After the war, some companies began to use plastic for dolls. Hard plastic seems to have been a good material for doll use. Relatively unbreakable, it seems not to deteriorate with time, such as the "magic skin" and other materials that were tried and discarded. The prime years of use (circa late 1940s – later 1950s) roughly a ten year period, produced a wide variety of beautiful dolls that Baby Boomers still remember fondly. With the advent of vinyl, in the late 50s and early 60s, less hard plastic dolls were made, although occasionally some manufacturer still presents hard plastic today.

Hard plastic, German, "Bavarian Bride," $225.00.
Courtesy Peggy Millhouse.

Hard plastic "Bride," $250.00.
Courtesy Sylvia Kleindinst.

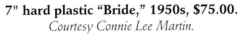

7" hard plastic "Bride," 1950s, $75.00.
Courtesy Connie Lee Martin.

All hard plastic, "Dorothy" doll, with play
wave set and saran hair, early 50s, take-off on
Ideal's Toni set, $200.00.
Courtesy Cathie Clark.

A hard plastic doll with movable eyes and arms,
a rocking chair and sewing accessories, Empire
Plastic Corporation, circa early 50s, $150.00.
Courtesy Cathie Clark.

Hard plastic "Dennis the Menace,"
raises gun and squirts water,
$140.00.
Courtesy Cathie Clark.

Hasbro

G.I. Joe

One of the developments in the doll field has been the action figure which has produced a whole series of doll collectors who prefer this type of doll. The most famous of those figures has to be G.I. Joe who has spawned a whole new era of collectors.

G.I. Joe, 1964 – 1976, 11½" tall.
Super Joes, 1976 – 1978, 8½" tall.
G.I. Joe, 1982 – on, 3½" tall.

JEM

Jem dolls were produced by Hasbro in 1985 and 1986. They were patterned after characters in the Jem cartoon television series which aired in 1985–1988 and was later available as reruns. The complete line of Jem dolls consists of only 21 dolls, but there are lots of variations and rare fashions to keep the collector hunting. All dolls are 12" tall (except Starlight who is 11") and totally posable as the knees and elbows bend, the waist and head turn, and the wrists swivel and are realistically proportioned like a human figure. They are made of vinyl with rooted hair. They are marked on head "Hasbro, Inc." and some backs are marked "COPYRIGHT 1985 HASBRO, INC//CHINA" and some are marked "COPYRIGHT 1987 HASBRO//MADE IN HONG KONG." Starlight girls are unmarked. The exciting thing about Jem dolls and the appeal to the public may have been the "truly outrageous" flashy mod fashions and startling hair colors available that made them so different from other fashion-type dolls of this era.

18" vinyl "Aimee," with long fat braid and jewelry, was called "The elegant doll with beautiful hair," $125.00.
Courtesy Cathie Clark.

Jem Dolls

"Aja" of the Holograms wearing
"Like A Dream" from the "Flip Side
Fashions," $35.00.
Courtesy Linda Holton.

"Aja" of the Holograms wearing
"Come On In" of the
"On Stage Fashions," $45.00.
Courtesy Linda Holton.

"Flash 'n Sizzle Jem" wearing
"Gettin' Down to Business" from
the "Flip Side Fashions," $30.00.
Courtesy Linda Holton.

12½" all vinyl, "Flash 'n Sizzle Jem"
wearing "Command Performance"
of the "On Stage Fashions," $40.00.
Courtesy Linda Holton.

Hasbro

12½" "Glitter 'n Gold Jem" wearing "Glitter 'n Gold Fashions,"
left: "Midnight Magic," $30.00,
center: "Golden Days Diamond Nights," $50.00,
right: "Purple Haze," $40.00.
Courtesy Linda Holton.

"Stormer" of the Misfits wearing:
left: "Designing Woman," $40.00,
right: "We're Off & Running" of the "Smashin'
Fashions," $35.00.
Courtesy Linda Holton.

"Glitter 'n Gold Fashions":
left: "Kimber" wearing "Fire & Ice," $45.00,
center: "Flash 'n Sizzle Jem" wearing "Moroccan Magic," $50.00,
right: "Shana" wearing "Gold Rush," $70.00.
Courtesy Linda Holton.

"Kimber," Jem's sister, wearing "Set
Your Sails" from the "On Stage Fashions," $25.00. *Courtesy Linda Holton.*

"Pizzazz" of the Misfits wearing:
left: **"You Gotta Be Fast" of the "Smashin' Fashions," $35.00,**
right: **"Gimme, Gimme, Gimme" of the "Smashin' Fashions," $35.00.**
Courtesy Linda Holton.

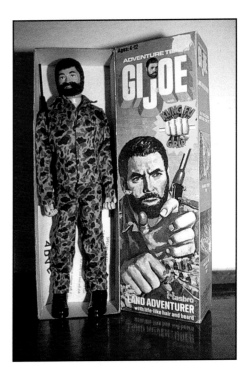

"G.I. Joe Land Adventurer"
in Army fatigues, $250.00.
Courtesy Cathie Clark.

18" vinyl "Sweet Cookie," comes with package of Jello Pudding, recipe book, and mixer, circa 1972, $125.00.
Courtesy Cathie Clark.

Hitty

Hitty is a character in the book, *Hitty, Her First Hundred Years* by Rachel Field, published in 1929. It is a story of a 6" doll, Hitty, and her adventures through 100 years. The story remains popular with people who read it as children and give the book to their children and grandchildren. It is charmingly illustrated with pen and ink drawings. Early editions also contain some color plates. The original Hitty makes her home in the Sturbridge, MA, library, while today's artists re-create Hitty for collectors. A Hitty newsletter is published and Hitty get-togethers happen at doll conventions and conferences.

Three 6" carved "Hitty" dolls by doll artist Pattie Hale, $300.00 ea.
Courtesy Pattie Hale.

Two 6" carved wooden "Hitty" dolls by doll artist Pattie Hale, $300.00 ea.
Courtesy Pattie Hale.

6" hand-carved, wooden "Hitty" doll
by Jeff Scott, jointed shoulders and
hips, wedding dress costume, $300.00.
Courtesy Rose Endrusick.

6" hand-carved, wooden "Hitty" doll
by Judy Brown, with painted features,
jointed arms and legs, dressed,
$225.00.
Private Collection.

6" hand-carved, wooden "Hitty" doll by
Helen Bullard, signed and numbered,
$350.00.
Courtesy Marilyn Ramsey.

6" hand-carved, wooden "Hitty" doll by Fred
Hahn, painted and dressed by Michele Simp-
son, jointed arms and legs, $185.00.
Courtesy Marilyn Ramsey.

Horsman

Horsman was founded by Edward Imeson Horsman in New York City. It operated from 1865 to 1980+. It merged with the Aetna Doll and Toy Company. Horsman distributed, assembled, and made dolls. In 1909 Horsman obtained his first copyright for a complete doll with Billiken. The company made hard plastic and vinyl dolls. Some of which are unmarked, some have only a number, and some are marked Horsman. Judds report painted inset pins on the walking mechanism is one means of identification of hard plastic dolls. The hard plastic dolls included "Cindy" with either a child or fashion-type body.

**Vinyl "Ice Cream," Bean Bag Goodies,
$35.00.**
Courtesy Cathie Clark.

12" composition "Campbell Kids," marked: "E.I.H.,"
circa 1910, $300.00 ea.
Courtesy Sherryl Shirran.

Vinyl head, "Bright Star,"
cloth body; Horsman's Shirley Temple
look-alike, circa 1989, $350.00.
Courtesy Angie Gonzales.

20" composition "Dimples," $300.00.
Courtesy McMasters Doll Auctions.

18" composition "Dimples," in tagged
original dress, molded painted hair,
cloth body with crier, $250.00.
Courtesy Janet Hill.

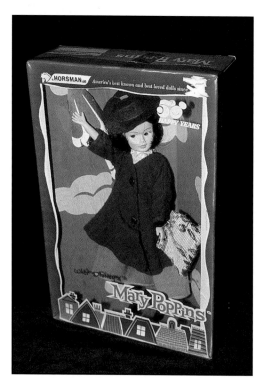

Foam filled vinyl "New Arrival" baby, $55.00.
Courtesy Cathie Clark.

Vinyl "Mary Poppins," labeled: "Happy
Years," circa 1964, $75.00+.
Courtesy Cathie Clark.

7¼" composition "Peek-A-Boo,"
with compo arms, legs, cloth body,
tagged, circa 1913 – 1915, licensed
by Grace G. Drayton, $125.00.
Courtesy Sherryl Shirran.

18" Rosebud, all original,
$250.00.

Courtesy Margie Welker.

26" composition "Sweetheart," $450.00.
Courtesy Margie Welker.

Composition "Sweetheart," re-dressed
$400.00.
Courtesy Helen Magill.

"Tessie Talker," all original
with box, $65.00.
Courtesy Cathie Clark.

Hoyer

Mary Hoyer Doll Mfg. Co.

Mary Hoyer operated a mail-order business and yarn shop and sold yarn and patterns for children's knitted and crocheted garments. She began to offer patterns for dolls and had Bernard Lipfert design a doll for her that was made first in composition and later in hard plastic. You could buy the doll undressed and make the patterned outfits for her. Hoyer also sold ready-made outfits. The dolls are marked "The Mary Hoyer Doll," or "ORIGINAL Mary Hoyer Doll." Today her granddaughter, Mary Lynne, carries on the business and produces dolls in vinyl based on an original book by Mary Hoyer, *The Doll with the Magic Wand*.

Hard plastic "Bride," $500.00.
Courtesy Gay Baron.

**14" Mary Hoyer doll,
crocheted dress, $400.00.**
Courtesy Angie Gonzales.

**14" composition Mary Hoyer doll,
$425.00.**
Courtesy Angie Gonzales.

**Vinyl Mary Hoyer souvenir doll from Mary Hoyer
Luncheon at the Modern Doll Convention, $275.00.**
Courtesy Marilyn Ramsey.

**14" all hard plastic, original tagged
outfit with box, circa 1950, $450.00.**
Courtesy Angie Gonzales

Left: Mary Hoyer attendant, $375.00;
right: composition, Effanbee "Suzanne Bride,"
$275.00.
Courtesy Sylvia Kleindinst.

18" hard plastic "Bride," "Bridesmaid," and "Mother of
Bride," all have tagged dressed, $500.00 ea.
Courtesy Gay Baron.

14" dolls, all marked with Mary Hoyer circle, $450.00 ea.
Courtesy Angie Gonzales.

Ideal

Ideal Novelty and Toy Co. produced their own composition dolls in the early years (1906–90+, Brooklyn, NY). Morris Michtom started the business by making teddy bears in 1906 with his wife, Rose, after the incident in which President Teddy Roosevelt would not shoot a bear cub during a hunting expedition. Michtom also began making composition "unbreakable" dolls about this time. His early comic characters were popular. Ideal also produced licensed dolls for companies to help promote their products such as Uneeda Kid that carried a small box of crackers for the Uneeda Biscuit Company. Some of their big successes were Shirley Temple in composition, Saucy Walker and Toni in hard plastic, and Miss Revlon in vinyl. They also made dolls of cloth and rubber. They used various marks including "IDEAL (in a diamond) USofA"; "IDEAL" Novelty and Toy Company, Brooklyn, New York"; and others.

10" and 11" vinyl "Who's On First?," Abbot and Costello in baseball uniforms, with cassette, 1984, $125.00 ea.
Courtesy Angie Gonzales.

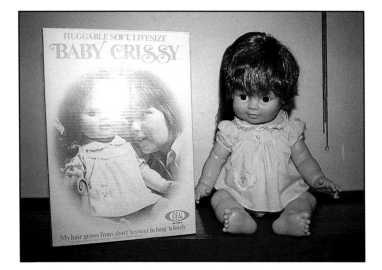

**24" vinyl "Baby Crissy," rooted grow hair,
circa 1973 – 1976, $200.00.**
Courtesy Cathie Clark.

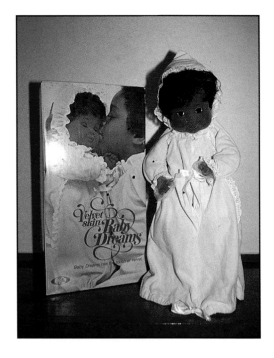

**17" vinyl "Baby Dreams,"
cloth body, arms and legs of magic
skin, rooted hair, 1975 – 1976, $75.00.**
Courtesy Cathie Clark.

**Composition "Betty Jane,"
with trunk and wardrobe,
$350.00.**
Courtesy Pat Schuda.

14" vinyl "Bonnie Braids,"
in original box, circa 1951, $175.00.
Courtesy Sherryl Shirran.

"Bonnie Braids," in box, the daughter of
comic strip character Dick Tracy, $175.00.
Courtesy Cathie Clark.

4½" vinyl "Flatsy Casey,"
wears engineer outfit, $25.00.
Courtesy Cathie Clark.

13" composition "Cinderella,"
on Shirley Temple body, $300.00.
Courtesy Eleanor Selmer.

Ideal

"Deanna Durbin," in red checked dress, box, pin, $650.00.
Courtesy Cathie Clark.

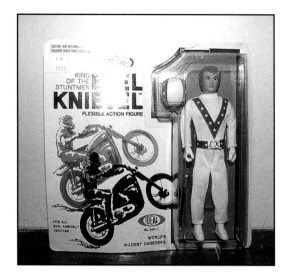

Action figure, motorcycle stuntman "Evel Knievel," $125.00.
Courtesy Cathie Clark.

17½" "Jewel Tressy," with accessories, $150.00.
Courtesy Cathie Clark.

15" vinyl "Harriet Hubbard Ayer," boxed, $200.00.
Courtesy McMasters Doll Auctions.

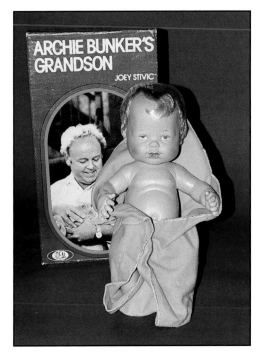

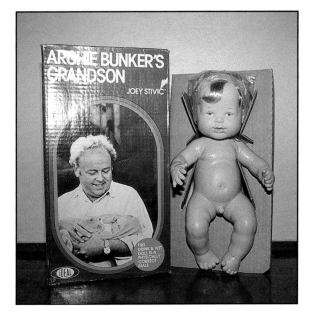

14" "Joey Stivic," Archie Bunker's grandson, box with blanket, two diapers, bottle, box states: "This drink and wet doll is a physically correct male," circa 1976, $100.00.
Courtesy Angie Gonzales.

14" vinyl "Joey Stivic," Archie Bunker's grandson, from TV sitcom, *All in the Family*, anatomically correct, 1976 – 1977, $100.00.
Courtesy Angie Gonzales.

12" all composition "Liberty Boy," jointed body with molded on clothes, replaced hat, $300.00.
Courtesy Marilyn Ramsey.

23" vinyl, "Kissy," all original, box and clothes, with Kissy label on dress, she puckers her lips and makes kissing noise when you press her arms together, circa 1961, $125.00.
Courtesy Angie Gonzales.

Ideal

**10½" "Little Miss Revlon," with box and brochure,
$125.00.**
Courtesy Cathie Clark.

**Vinyl Sara Stimson as "Little Miss Marker,"
in remake of Shirley Temple movie, $45.00.**
Private Collection.

**10½" vinyl "Little Miss Revlon,"
MIB, $125.00.**
Courtesy Cathie Clark.

**16" all original, hard plastic "Mary Hartline,"
with eyeshadow over eyes, marked "P-91,"
$400.00.**
Courtesy Sally McVey.

20" vinyl "Miss Revlon," boxed, $250.00.
Courtesy McMasters Doll Auctions

20" vinyl "Miss Revlon," boxed, $250.00.
Courtesy McMasters Doll Auctions.

Vinyl "Miss Revlon"
in "Cherries a la Mode" dress,
$275.00.
Courtesy Cathie Clark.

15" vinyl head, hard plastic body,
"Miss Revlon," tagged floral dress,
with Revlon brochure, $200.00.
Courtesy Sally McVey.

Ideal

"Patti Playful," can be manipulated
with hand in back, $150.00.
Courtesy Cathie Clark.

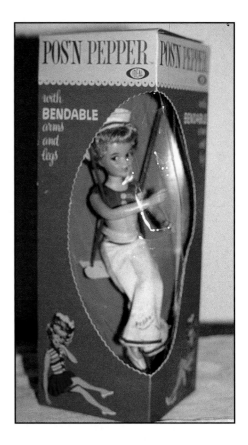

Vinyl "Pos'n Pepper,"
with bendable arms and legs, $75.00.
Courtesy Cathie Clark.

17" vinyl, black "Rub-A-Dub Dolly,"
water tight, can bathe with you, 1979,
$125.00.
Courtesy Cathie Clark.

23" vinyl "Posie" walking doll, bent
knees, rooted saran hair, $175.00.
Courtesy Cathie Clark.

12" "Tammy," vinyl head and arms, hard plastic body,
extra wardrobe, 1962, $75.00.
Courtesy Cathie Clark.

17" vinyl, black "Wake Up Thumbelina,"
turns over, battery operated, $125.00.
Courtesy Cathie Clark.

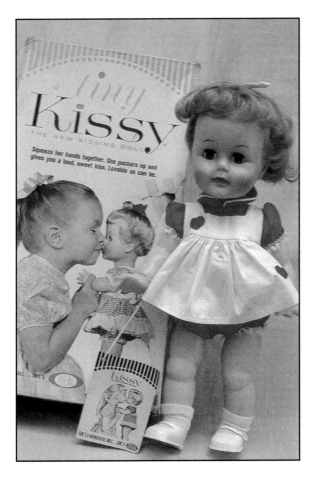

16" vinyl "Tiny Kissy," pull arms together she
puckers lips, circa 1963 – 1968, $150.00.
Courtesy Cathie Clark.

"Thumbelina Toddler,"
has her own walker, $75.00.
Courtesy Cathie Clark.

14" hard plastic "Toni," $600.00.
Courtesy McMasters Doll Auctions.

21" hard plastic "Toni," marked "P-93," original outfit, eyeshadow above eyes, pretty coloring, $650.00. *Courtesy Bev Mitchell.*

15" hard plastic "Toni," blue sleep eyes, closed mouth, red nylon hair, all original, hang-tag, tagged pink jumper, $375.00+.
Courtesy Stephanie Prince.

14" hard plastic "Toni,"
all original with tagged dress, box with play
wave set, circa 1948, $350.00.
Courtesy Angie Gonzales.

21" hard plastic "Toni," boxed, $650.00.
Courtesy McMasters Doll Auctions.

21" hard plastic "Toni," lovely color, original outfit, tag,
and Toni playwave box, marked "P-93," $550.00.
Courtesy Sally McVey.

**11½" "Tuesday Taylor" and her boyfriend, "Eric,"
$65.00.**
Courtesy Cathie Clark.

**Hard plastic "Toni Bride,"
complete with box, play wave, and tag, $650.00.**
Courtesy Cathie Clark.

Kenner

The *Star Wars* movie was made in 1977, and the sequel *The Empire Strikes Back* in 1980. Kenner made large Star Wars figures in 1978 in Hong Kong, ranging in height from 7" to 15". They included Princess Leia Organa, Luke Sykwalker, R2-D2, Chewbaca, Darth Vader, and C-3P0. In 1979 Boba Fett, Han Solo, Stormtrooper, Ben (Obi-Wan) Kenobi, Jawa, and IG-88 were added. They also made 3 – 4" small figures starting in 1979.

Vinyl action figure "Bob Scout," with Boy Scout uniform and accessories, $45.00.
Courtesy Cathie Clark.

12" vinyl "Dusty" the golf champion, $45.00.
Courtesy Cathie Clark.

12" "Dr. Hugo" hand puppet, "Man of a Thousand Faces," $75.00.
Courtesy Cathie Clark.

Klumpe

Klumpe made caricature figures of felt over wire armature with painted mask faces in Barcelona, Spain, from 1952 to the mid 1970s. Figures represent professionals, hobbyists, Spanish dancers, historical characters, and contemporary males and females performing a wide variety of tasks. Of the 200 or more different figures, the most common are Spanish dancers, bull fighters, and doctors. Some Klumpes were imported by Effanbee in the early 50s. Originally the figures had two sewn-on identifying cardboard tags.

**Felt dancer with top hat and cane,
circa 1960, $95.00.**
Courtesy Sondra Gast.

Felt "Napoleon," circa 1960, $105.00.
Courtesy Sondra Gast.

Felt "Traveling Girl,"
with typical gold/red foil paper label,
circa 1960, $110.00.
Courtesy Sondra Gast.

Knickerbocker

Knickerbocker Toy Co. Inc. has made a variety of celebrity dolls among others. The celebrities include two versions of Annie, from the stage play based on "Little Orphan Annie," and Daddy Warbucks, Punjab, Miss Hannigan, and Molly; Laura and Carrie from the TV version of Laura Ingalls Wilder's *Little House on the Prairie*; Mr. Spock and Captain Kirk from *Star Trek;* and comedians Laurel and Hardy, W.C. Fields, and Soupy Sales. One version of Annie is based on the actress Andrea McArdle, circa 1977. It is a 15" all cloth doll with jointed arms and legs, orange yarn hair, painted features, and her dog Sandy in the pocket of her red dress.

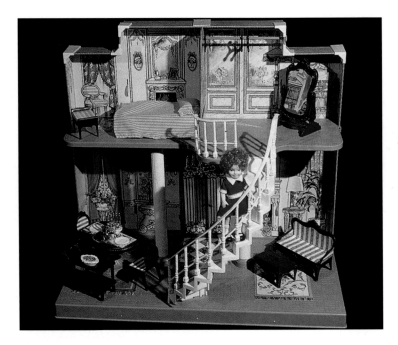

"Little Orphan Annie," a vinyl celebrity doll from the musical that starred Aileen Quinn as Annie, shown in her mansion, 1982, $65.00.
Courtesy Cathie Clark.

Lawton

Wendy Lawton was born in San Francisco and attended and graduated from California schools. There, she met her husband, Keith, married, and made her home in Turlock, California, with their two children, Rebecca and Patrick. Her interests have developed around her home and her own artistic achievements and was guided early on by doll maker, Thelma Hanke, who taught her all phases of doll making including making wigs, costuming, and fabrics.

Wendy is an avid reader and has been inspired by children's literature and classics to bring to life her own dolls. The family company has greatly expanded, but is still overseen by Wendy who designs, sculpts, and paints all prototypes, designs their costumes, and does some painting on the final dolls. Wendy enjoys the challenge of researching each new subject by reading and conceptualizing the character before designing the doll. Lawton's Josephine, the souvenir doll for the UFDC Region 2 North Conference in Modesto, was a big hit, and quickly more than doubled the registration fee in price. The companion piece was a suitcase with extra garments, exquisitely made, as are all of the special accessories that accompany Lawton dolls.

Lawton was a 1996 DOTY Award nominee for Katherine and her Kathe Kruse Doll, Phoebe Preble and Hitty, June Amos and Mary Anne, and The Scarlet Letter. See Collectors' Network for information on the Lawton Collectors Guild.

"Britta," porcelain, limited edition of 100, $595.00.
Courtesy Toni Winder.

"Karen," limited edition of 50
for Disney World, $800.00.
Courtesy Toni Winder.

"Rose," porcelain, with music box in
tummy, 1987, $250.00+.
Courtesy Toni Winder.

"Lotta Crabtree," porcelain, first convention doll,
limited edition of 125, $1,300.00.
Courtesy Toni Winder.

14" all porcelain, "Snow White,"
1993, limited edition of 500,
$400.00.

Second WL convention doll,
"Through the Looking Glass,"
$1,100.00.
Courtesy Toni Winder.

Marx

Louis Marx & Co., Inc.

Marx began by making tin mechanical toys, later they made sets with numerous small plastic figures, and still later articulated figures of rigid vinyl, including the Johnny West action figures, circa 1965 – 1975. These were advertised in Sears catalogs. Other articulated figures made by Marx include celebrities Daniel Boone, Davy Crockett, Dwight D. Eisenhower, General Custer, Geronimo, and the Sundown Kid.

11½" rigid vinyl, articulated figure "Sam Cobra," an outlaw, with 26 accessories in box, $125.00.
Courtesy Chad Moyer.

9" rigid vinyl, articulated figure "Jay West," blond hair, and molded on clothing, 13 accessories, with box, $40.00.
Courtesy Chad Moyer.

9" rigid vinyl, articulated figure "Janice West,"
molded on clothing, and 14 accessories
including vinyl removable clothing, $40.00.
Courtesy Carol Hager.

11½" rigid vinyl, articulated figure "Princess
Wildflower," from Johnny West's Best of the West
Series, with papoose in vinyl cradle, 22 accessories,
came with either orange or turquoise vinyl clothing,
$125.00.
Courtesy Chad Moyer.

Mattel, Inc.

Mattel was founded in 1945, in Los Angeles, CA, and has been a indominable force in the doll industry with their Barbie, Chatty Cathy, and others. Ruth and Elliott Handler and friend, Harold Matson, founded the Mattel company, Matt for Matson and el for Elliot. They first made picture frames, and evolved into toy furniture. Mattson left the company because of ill health and Ruth Handler began to handle marketing. She advertised in 1955 on *The Mickey Mouse Club*. In 1959, they marketed a fashion doll named after their daughter, and the company prospered. They also have manufactured quite a list of celebrity dolls as well as characters from TV shows. (See also Barbie.)

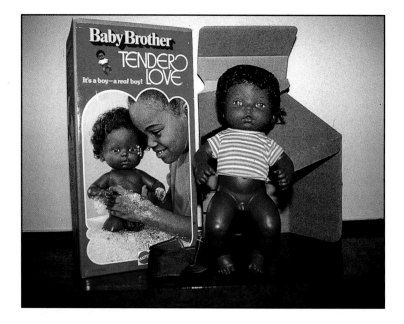

Vinyl, "Baby Brother Tender Love," anatomically correct, $65.00.
Courtesy Cathie Clark.

**18" vinyl "Baby First Step," circa 1964,
$27.00.**
Courtesy Cathie Clark.

**18" "Baby First Step,"
walks and roller skates, $25.00.**
Courtesy Cathie Clark.

**Vinyl "Baby Love Light," her eyes light
up when you hold her hand, battery
operated, circa 1970, $20.00.**
Courtesy Cathie Clark.

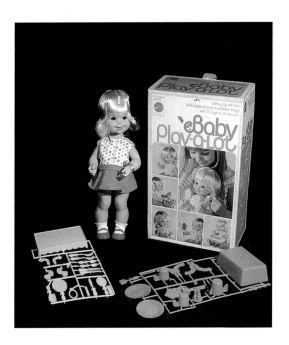

**16" vinyl "Baby Play-a-lot,"
with 20 accessories, circa 1971, $22.00.**
Courtesy Cathie Clark.

Mattel, Inc.

**15" vinyl "Cathy Quick Curl," with
brush and comb, $50.00.**
Courtesy Cathie Clark.

**25" vinyl "Charmin' Chatty,"
circa 1961, $225.00.**
Courtesy Cathie Clark.

Talking "Chatty Baby," $150.00.
Courtesy Cathie Clark.

**20" "Chatty Cathy," $300.00;
with Chatty Cathy stroller $150.00.**
Courtesy Cathie Clark.

"Singing Chatty," circa 1964, $150.00.
Courtesy Cathie Clark.

**15" "Tiny Chatty Baby,"
circa 1963, $150.00.**
Courtesy Cathie Clark.

**"Cynthia," a high heel doll,
circa 1971, $125.00.**
Courtesy Cathie Clark.

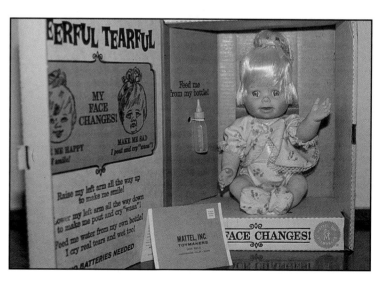

**"Cheerful Tearful," changes expressions when you move
her arms, a drink and wet doll, circa 1965, $125.00.**
Courtesy Cathie Clark.

"Liddle Red Ridding Hiddle,"
1967 – 1968, $85.00.
Courtesy Paris Langford.

Liddle Kiddles sticker pictures, 1968,
$55.00.
Courtesy Paris Langford.

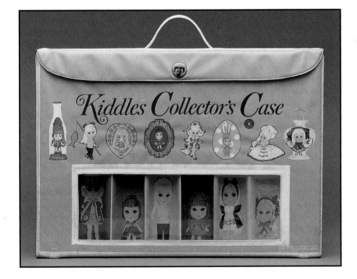

Liddle Kiddles pink collector's case, 1968, $25.00.
Courtesy Paris Langford.

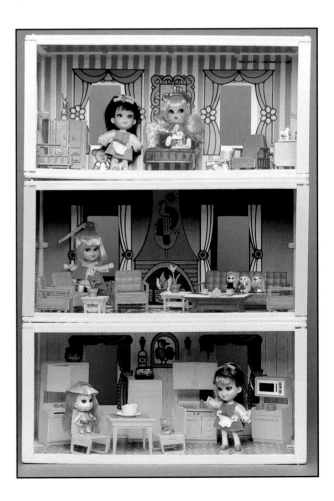

Liddle Kiddles Playhouse
"Kiddles 'n Friends," 1970.
Three snap together sets:
"Cookin' Hiddle," $95.00,
"Pretty Parlor," $95.00,
"Good-Night Kiddle," $95.00.
Courtesy Paris Langford.

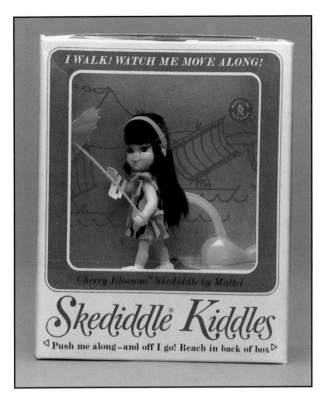

"Alice In Wonderliddle,"
Storybook Kiddles, 1968, MIB, $100.00.
Courtesy Paris Langford.

"Skediddle Kiddles Cherry Blossom,"
MIB, $75.00.
Courtesy Paris Langford.

Cloth "Mrs. Beasley" from TV sitcom
***A Family Affair,* $50.00.**
Courtesy Cathie Clark.

"Rosebud," $50.00.
Courtesy Cathie Clark.

"Pioneer Daughter," Star Spangled
Dolls, uses Sunshine Family bodies,
circa 1976, $45.00.
Courtesy Cathie Clark.

15" vinyl "Saucy,"
makes faces, circa 1972, $225.00.
Courtesy Cathie Clark.

12" vinyl "Donny and Marie Osmond,"
with extra outfits, $50.00 ea.
Courtesy Cathie Clark.

20" "Swingy," dances and turns,
comes with record, $50.00.
Courtesy Cathie Clark.

19" vinyl "Sketchy,"
with drawing desk, draws 11 things,
no batteries needed, $125.00.
Courtesy Cathie Clark.

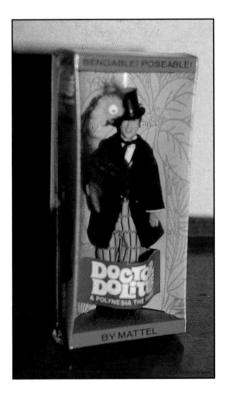

6" vinyl "Dr. Doolittle," $50.00.
Courtesy Cathie Clark.

11½" vinyl
"Talking Stacey,"
in box, $150.00.
Courtesy Cathie Clark.

16" vinyl "Tippee Toes," can ride her
trike or pony, circa 1967, $125.00.
Courtesy Cathie Clark.

Mego

Mego Corp. made a huge slate of action figures, comic figures, and celebrity dolls including the "Our Gang" characters; Batman, Robin, the Joker and Batgirl; Dorothy, The Tinman, The Cowardy Lion, and Scarecrow from *The Wizard of Oz;* The Captain and Tenille; Diana Ross; Davy Crockett; Captain James Kirk, Dr. McCoy, Mr. Spock, Mr. Scott, and Lt. Uhura; Farah Fawcett; Flash Gordon; Glinda the Good Witch; Broadway Joe Namath; Buck Rogers; Johnboy and the *Waltons* characters; *M.A.S.H.* characters; *Happy Days* characters, Ritche, Ralph, and Fonzie; Superman; Spiderman; Wild Bill Hickok; and Wonder Woman.

12" "Cher" with some of her packaged fashions, $45.00+.
Courtesy Cathie Clark.

**11½" vinyl "Dorothy Hamill,"
Olympic skating star, $40.00.**
Courtesy Cathie Clark.

**12½" vinyl "Farrah Fawcett," model,
TV, and movie personality, $45.00.**
Courtesy Cathie Clark.

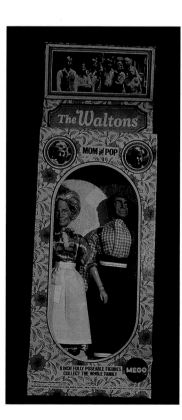

**6" "Our Gang" set, complete with club house
and accessories, circa 1975, $1,000.00 set.**
Courtesy Cathie Clark.

**"Mom and Pop," from *The
Waltons* TV show, circa 1975, $35.00.**
Courtesy Cathie Clark.

"Ralph," from *Happy Days*
TV show, $15.00.
Courtesy Cathie Clark.

12¼" vinyl "Suzanne Sommers,"
as Chrissy from TV sitcom
Three's Company, $28.00.
Courtesy Cathie Clark.

12" posable "Sonny & Cher," TV
personalities, $75.00.
Courtesy Cathie Clark.

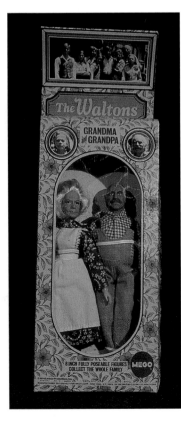

"Grandma and Grandpa Walton,"
from the TV show *The Waltons,*
circa 1975, $35.00.
Courtesy Cathie Clark.

12½" vinyl "Wonder Woman," comic book and TV
character played by Lynda Carter, circa 1975, $150.00.
Courtesy Cathie Clark.

Multi-face or Multi-head

Whatever whimsical mood has prompted doll artists to make dolls with more than one face, or more than one head, the results seem to always amuse and appeal to the collector. Made of various materials by many different manufacturers, these are grouped together to show some examples. Some collectors choose to focus a whole collection around them, and surely every collector will want to have at least one example.

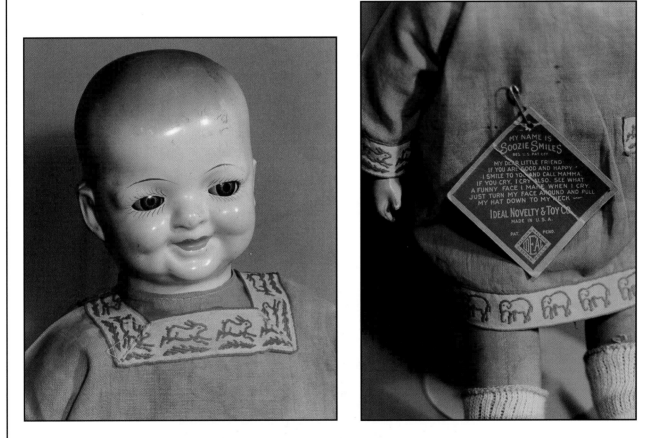

**Ideal's "Soozie Smiles," two faces, one crying,
the other smiling, with sleep eyes, original dress, tag, missing hat, $350.00.**
Courtesy Marilyn Ramsey.

Munich Art Dolls

From 1908 to the 1920s, Marion Kaulitz painted doll faces on heads by several designers. They were then dressed by others. They usually had composition heads with wigs, painted eyes, and ball jointed composition bodies. Sometimes Cuno and Otto Dressel bodies were used. They were often dressed in German or French regional costumes. They were distributed in the U.S. by Arnoldt Doll Co. Occasionally one of these delightful dolls turns up at auction.

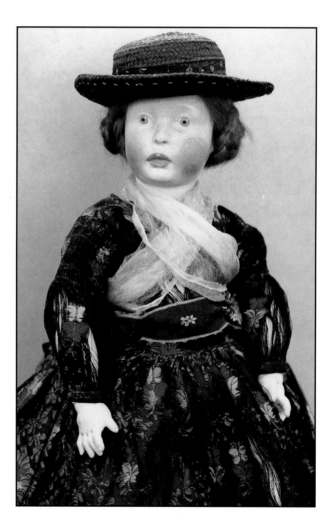

**19" composition, Munich Art Doll
by Marion Kaulitz, original costume deteriorating,
circa 1908 – 1912, $2,000.00+.**
Courtesy Sherryl Shirran.

Nancy Ann Storybook Dolls, Inc.

Nancy Ann Storybook Dolls, Inc. was started by Rowena Haskin (Nancy Ann Abbott) in 1936, in San Francisco, CA. The dolls were painted bisque with mohair wigs and painted eyes. Their heads were molded to their torsos, and they had jointed limbs. They either had a sticker on their outfit or hangtag. They also made a hard plastic 8" Muffie and 18" Miss Nancy Ann Style Show, and an 11" Debbie and 7½" Lori Ann with vinyl heads and hard plastic bodies. In the 1950s and 1960s they made 10½" Miss Nancy Ann and Little Miss Nancy Ann, vinyl high heeled fashion-type dolls.

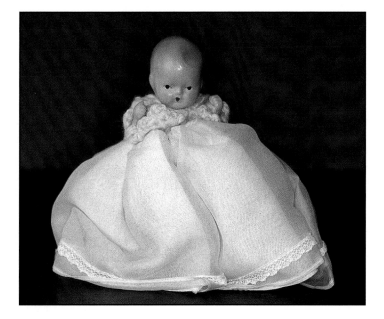

**Nancy Ann Storybook, painted bisque, 4½" "Baby,"
closed fist, long dress and crocheted jacket, $125.00.**
Courtesy Elaine Pardee.

Nancy Ann Story Book Dolls, Inc.

5" bisque "Black-eyed Susan" from the Flower series, jointed arms and legs, pudgy tummy, $250.00.
Courtesy Elaine Pardee.

9" vinyl "Baby Sue Sue," molded hair, marked "Nancy Ann," tagged clothes, $75.00.
Courtesy Elaine Pardee.

Hard plastic "Debbie," all original with box, $170.00.
Courtesy Elaine Pardee.

All bisque "Chinese" Around the World Series, marked "Storybook Doll USA11," $750.00.
Courtesy Elaine Pardee.

**Hard plastic, Nancy Ann Style Show
"Demure Miss," face only, $600.00.**
Courtesy Elaine Pardee.

**Vinyl "Debbie Walker," button in back,
with box, $90.00.**
Courtesy Elaine Pardee.

**Hard plastic "#12 Easter Parade,"
black sleep eye, Hit Parade Series, $125.00.**
Courtesy Elaine Pardee.

**Nancy Ann Storybook, #1006 NASB Sofa,
$150.00.**
Courtesy Elaine Pardee.

Nancy Ann Story Book Dolls, Inc.

Hard plastic "Goes to Party," from Big and Little
Sister Series, sleep eyes, $65.00.
Courtesy Elaine Pardee.

5" bisque "Hansel & Gretel," from the Storybook Series,
jointed arms and legs, molded socks, $425.00 pair.
Courtesy Elaine Pardee.

All bisque "Italian," Around the World Series,
marked "Made In Japan 1146,"
$500.00. *Courtesy Elaine Pardee.*

Vinyl "Lori Ann," Dutch cut, unmarked,
$165.00.
Courtesy Elaine Pardee.

5" bisque "Margie Ann," jointed arms
and legs, in hat and coat from the
Family Series, has molded socks and
white boots. $150.00.
Private Collection.

8" "Lori Ann," vinyl head,
hard plastic body, $165.00.
Courtesy Elaine Pardee.

Hard plastic "Miss Nancy Ann," #342 Formal Affair
styles, tagged dress, marked "Nancy" on back of
head, $125.00.
Courtesy Elaine Pardee.

Hard plastic "Miss Nancy Ann,"
tagged outfit, $125.00.
Courtesy Elaine Pardee.

Hard plastic "Muffie,"
in Graduation outfit," $80.00.
Courtesy Elaine Pardee.

Hard plastic "Muffie Walker," in original
box, marked "Story Book Dolls California
Muffie," $160.00.
Courtesy Elaine Pardee.

17½" hard plastic
"Nancy Ann Styleshow," $350.00.
Courtesy Sally McVey.

6½" hard plastic "New Moon" from the Operetta Series,
painted eyes, $125.00.
Courtesy Elaine Pardee.

7" "Princess Monon Minette" and "Prince Souci,"
from In Powder and Crinoline Series,
jointed arms and legs, $165.00 ea.
Courtesy Elaine Pardee.

5" hard plastic, Nancy Ann "Red Riding Hood"
and "Queen of Hearts" dolls, $40.00 ea.
Courtesy Angie Gonzales.

5" "Russian" from the Around the
World Series, bisque, jointed arms
and legs, has molded socks and
white boots, $450.00.
Courtesy Elaine Pardee.

5" hard plastic "Queen of Hearts,"
$35.00.
Courtesy Bev Mitchell.

Nancy Ann Story Book Dolls, Inc.

5" painted bisque, Nancy Ann Story Book, all original with gold paper wrist tag, circa 1930, $150.00.
Courtesy Pidd Miller.

5" "Skier" from the Sports Series, bisque, jointed arms and legs, has molded socks, $600.00.
Courtesy Elaine Pardee.

Nancy Ann Style Show, "Lavender and Lace," hard plastic, face only, $50.00.
Courtesy Elaine Pardee.

Puppets and Marionettes

Left: composition, "Mr. Bluster," $450.00,
right: 14" "Dilly Dally,"
made by Peter Puppet Playthings, Inc.,
designed by Raye Copelan, $495.00.
Both in original boxes.
Courtesy McMasters Doll Auction.

Left: 16½" composition "Captain
Hook," $200.00,
left center: 14½" "Peter Pan,"
$225.00,
right center: 14" "Wendy," $225.00,
right: 14" "Indian," $175.00.

**Marionettes are made by Peter Puppet Playthings, Inc.,
and designed by Ray Copelan.**
Courtesy McMasters Doll Auction.

Quintuplets

Alexander Doll Co. won the license to produce the official Dionne Quintuplets after their birth in 1934 to a Canadian farm couple. Designed by Bernard Lipfert, they were all composition, with painted eyes, molded hair, and jointed baby bodies. They were also made as toddlers in different sizes. Not to be outdone, other companies came out with their own sets of five babies to try to hitch on to the selling frenzy that followed the quintuplets fame. Quint collectors have their own newsletter and collect all sorts of related memorabilia as well as the dolls. See Collectors' Network for information on the *Quint News*.

Composition, Madame Alexander,
"Dionne Quintuplets," $900.00.
Courtesy Cherie Gervais.

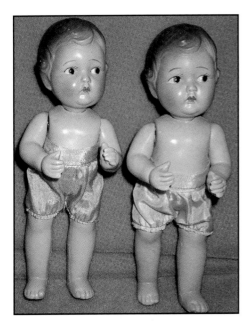

7" composition, Japanese quints, circa 1936, $750.00 set.
Courtesy Connie Lee Martin.

7½" composition, Japanese quints, $750.00.
Courtesy Connie Lee Martin.

Japanese, composition, quint toddlers, $1,000.00.
Courtesy Connie Lee Martin.

19" composition, Madame Alexander, "Emily," Dionne Quint toddler, $750.00+.
Courtesy Marian Pettygrove.

7½" composition, Madame Alexander "Dionne Quintuplets," $1,000.00.
Courtesy McMasters Doll Auctions.

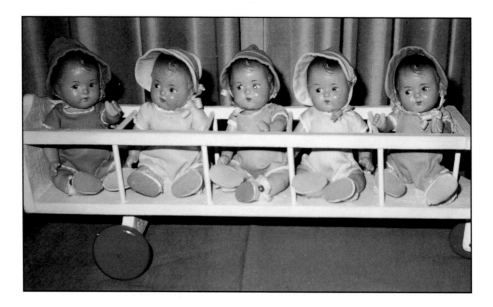

Composition, Madame Alexander "Dionne Quintuplets," $1,200.00.
Courtesy Dorothy Doring.

14" composition, Madame Alexander
"Yvonne," Dionne Quint, $350.00+.
Courtesy Marilyn Moran.

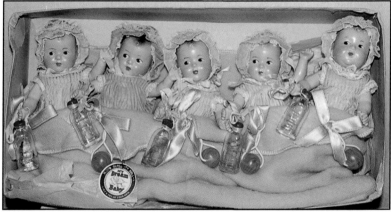

Composition, Arranbee quintuplets,
$1,000.00.
Courtesy Georgia Henry.

Composition, Madame Alexander
"Dionne Quintuplets, $1,400.00;
& Dr. Dafoe," $1,200.00.
Courtesy Georgia Henry.

Quintuplets

Seven, 4" composition "Days of the Week Babies," box says the "7-day Babies," marked Japan, $500.00 set.
Courtesy Connie Lee Martin.

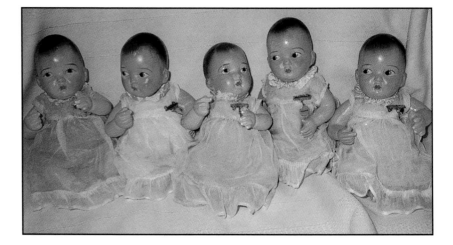

6½" Japanese, composition, all original except for name pins, $675.00.
The brown eyes are painted differently, more like character faces. They have chubby bent limb bodies.
Courtesy Connie Lee Martin.

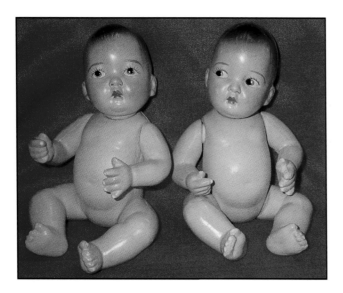

6½" Japanese, composition, all original except for name pins, $675.00.
The brown eyes are painted differently, more like character faces. They have chubby bent limb bodies.
Courtesy Connie Lee Martin.

Left: 14" composition, Alexander "Dr. Dafoe," tagged suit, hat, $1,400.00.
right: 13" composition, Alexander "Nurse," tagged dress and cap, $875.00.
Courtesy McMasters Doll Auctions.

Five 7½" composition, Alexander "Dionne Quintuplets," in tagged sunsuits and bonnets, suitcase with fancy dresses, $3,800.00.
Courtesy McMasters Doll Auctions.

7" composition, Effanbee quints, a take-off of the Alexander Dionne Quintuplets, in box with extra kimono and diaper, circa 1935, $2,000.00.
Courtesy Marilyn Ramsey.

7" composition, Effanbee quint, one of a set of five dressed in different pastel organdy dresses, painted eyes, painted molded hair, $1,750.00.
These were advertised just as quints in 1935 to take advantage of the popular Dionne Quintuplets.
Courtesy Marilyn Ramsey.

Raggedy Ann & Andy

Designed by Johnny Gruelle in 1915, made by various companies. Ann wears dress with apron, Andy shirt and pants with matching hat.

P.J. Volland, 1920–1934, early dolls marked "Patented Sept. 7, 1915." All cloth, tin or wooden button eyes, painted features. Some have sewn knee or arm joints, sparse brown or auburn yarn hair, oversize hands, feet turned outward.

Mollye Goldman, 1935–38

Marked on chest: "Raggedy Ann and Andy Dolls Manufactured by Mollye's Doll Outfitters." Nose outlined in black, red heart on chest, reddish orange hair, multicolored legs, blue feet, some have oilcloth faces.

Georgene Novelties, 1938–62

Ann has orange hair and a top knot, six different mouth styles, early dolls had tin eyes, later plastic, six different noses, seams in middle of legs and arms to represent knees and elbows, feet turn forward, red and white striped legs. All have hearts that say "I love you" printed on chest. Tag sewn to left side seam, several variations, all say "Georgene Novelties, Inc."

Knickerbocker, 1962–82

Printed features, hair color changes from orange to red; there were five mouth and eyelash variations, tags were located on clothing back or pant seam.

Applause Toy Company, 1981–83, Hasbro (Playskool) 1983+

Raggedy Ann storybooks and dolls remain a favorite with doll collectors. They too, have a newsletter *Rags* devoted to collectors, see Collectors' Network for more information.

19" Georgene "Raggedy Andy," with black
outlined nose, circa 1938 – 1945,
$1,000.00.
Courtesy Sherryl Shirran.

16" cloth, Volland "Raggedy Ann,"
$400.00.
Courtesy McMasters Doll Auctions.

18" cloth, Mollye's
"Raggedy Andy," $425.00.
Courtesy McMasters Doll Auctions.

Raggedy Ann & Andy

16" cloth, Volland "Raggedy Ann," $850.00,
30" bisque K*R child, $850.00.
Courtesy McMasters Doll Auctions.

19" Georgene "Raggedy Ann," with black
outlined nose, circa 1938 – 1945, $1,000.00.
Courtesy Sherryl Shirran.

**Two Georgene Averill, cloth
"Raggedy Ann & Andy" dolls
tagged, $195.00.**
Courtesy Marilyn Ramsey.

Remco

Remco Industries (ca. 1960–74) was one of the first companies to market with television ads.

Littlechap Family

Introduced in 1963, these dolls had vinyl heads and arms, rooted hair, painted molded features, and hard vinyl bodies. The Littlechaps were an upper-class American family with the father a doctor, member of the Lanesville County Medical Society, former flight surgeon of the U.S. Army Air Force. Dr. John, 15", "loves his family and golf." Wife, Lisa Littlechap, 15", is president of the local PTA, a wonderful cook, former model, and always elegantly dressed. Big sister, Judy Littlechap, 13½", is a seventeen-year-old senior and an honor student at Lanesville High School, naturally loves parties and crazy desserts. Libby Littlechap, 10½", is the kid sister of the family, ten years old, in the 5th grade at Lanesville Elementary, and loves to climb tress, pester her big sister, and wants to grow up to be a doctor like her father.

Marked on their backs in a circle "Littlechap//Remco Industries//c 1963." Outfits were available separately, including winter outerwear, suits, evening clothes, beach wear, day dresses, lingerie, nightclothes, and sportswear.

One of the Beatles, "Ringo Star,"
$200.00.
Courtesy Cathie Clark.

5" vinyl "Heidi," in plastic case, circa
1965, $35.00.
Courtesy Angie Gonzales.

16" vinyl, Remco "Baby Laugh a Lot,"
comes with a vinyl rocker, $65.00.
Courtesy Cathie Clark.

"Jeannie," of the TV sitcom *I Dream of Jeannie,* all vinyl,
she also has her bottle and accessories,
circa 1966, $150.00.
Courtesy Cathie Clark.

"Herman Munster," seven foot tall
character from TV sitcom, *The Mun-
sters,* 1964 – 1966, played by actor
Fred Gwynne, $250.00.
Courtesy Cathie Clark.

Richwood

Richwood Toys, Inc., was located in Annapolis, MD. Sandra Sue was produced from the late forties through the fifties.

Sandra Sue had sleep eyes with molded lashes, closed mouth, jointed arms and legs, made as a walker and non-walker, and had an extensive wardrobe as well as a line of furniture. She had saran wigs, a suggestion of a fashion body with gently molded breasts and a slimmer waist. She was modeled with both flat and high heel feet. One tip for identification is dark orange painted eyebrows and painted lashes below eyes. The only mark is a number under the arm or leg. The hands are formed with fingers together and separate thumbs, and the palms face the body.

Sandra Sue's head did not turn when she walked. Her wardrobe, which could be purchased separately, would be the envy of many of the contemporary dolls. This included evening and bridal gowns, sportswear such as ski apparel and skating costumes, skirts and blouses, dresses and hats, coat and dress ensembles with accessories, daytime dresses, and more. Sandra Sue's original box is easily recognizable with a silhouette in an oval and her name marked on top.

Ad for "Sandra Sue,"
in 1952 *House Beautiful* magazine.
Courtesy Peggy Millhouse.

Sandra Sue furniture, bed with finals, bedding complete, $50.00 – 100.00; dining table with extension and two chairs, $50.00 – 100.00; and vanity with skirt, mirror, and chair, $35.00 – $75.00.
Courtesy Peggy Millhouse.

8" hard plastic "Sandra Sue," C-14, high heel, in skirt and blouse, $175.00.
Courtesy Peggy Millhouse.

8" hard plastic "Sandra Sue Bride," high heel walker, circa 1955, $200.00+.
Courtesy Peggy Millhouse.

8" hard plastic "Sandra Sue," flat foot walker, in classic slip and camisole, $175.00.
Courtesy Peggy Millhouse.

8" hard plastic "Sandra Sue," flat foot walker, #41 taffeta rooster tail dress, replaced hat, circa 1954, $200.00.
Courtesy Peggy Millhouse

8" hard plastic, H-15, "Sandra Sue," replaced ballet slippers, circa 1953, $125.00.
Courtesy Peggy Millhouse.

8" hard plastic, flat foot "Sandra Sue" walkers, two skirt and blouse sets, replaced non-Sandra Sue shoes, $300.00 pair.
Courtesy Peggy Millhouse

8" hard plastic "Sandra Sue Majorette,"
flat foot walker, $150.00.
Courtesy Peggy Millhouse.

8" flat-footed "Sandra Sue Skier,"
$125.00.
Courtesy Peggy Millhouse.

8" hard plastic "Sandra Sue," from the high heel brochure, F-70, in red and white long gown, $200.00.
Courtesy Peggy Millhouse.

8" hard plastic "Sandra Sue," high heel non-walker, $125.00.
Courtesy Peggy Millhouse.

Roldan

Roldan Characters are similar to Klumpe figures in many respects. They were made in Barcelona, Spain, from the early 1960s until the mid 1970s. They are made of felt over a wire armature, with painted mask faces. Like Klumpe, Roldan figures represent professionals, hobbyists, dancers, historical characters, and contemporary males and females performing a wide variety of tasks. Some, but not all Roldans, were imported by Rosenfield Imports and Leora Dolores of Hollywood. Figures originally came with two, sewn-on, identifying cardboard tags. Roldan characters most commonly found are doctors, Spanish dancers, and bull fighters. Characters tend to have somewhat smaller heads, longer necks, and more defined facial features than Klumpe.

Felt "Traveling Lady," circa 1965, $95.00.
Courtesy Sondra Gast.

Sasha

Sasha dolls were created by Swiss artist, Sasha Morgenthaler, who hand-crafted 20" children and 13" babies in Zurich, Switzerland, from the 1940s until her death in 1975. Her handmade studio dolls had cloth or molded bodies, five different head molds, and were hand painted by Sasha Morgenthaler. To make her dolls affordable as children's playthings, she licensed Gotz Puppenfabrik (1964 – 1970) in Germany and Frido Trendon Ltd. (1965 – 1986) in England to manufacture 16" Sasha doll in series. The manufactured dolls were made of rigid vinyl with painted features. Gotz Dolls, Inc. was granted a new license in 1994, and is currently producing them in Germany. See Collectors' Network for more information on the Sasha newsletter.

16" rigid vinyl "Sasha,"
in box with straw hat, $250.00.
Courtesy Cathie Clark.

Two early 16" Frido-Trendon Ltd., "Sasha" red-haired dolls, in "Ballet" and "Dungarees" outfits, circa 1966 – 1968. $600.00 – 1,000.00. Mint in box prices range up to $1000.00 each depending on outfit for this era dolls. Dolls less pristine will bring much lower prices.
Courtesy Dorisanne Osborn.

16" "Sasha," "Pinafore" outfit, Frido-Trendon Ltd., circa 1980s, $250.00.
Courtesy Dorisanne Osborn.

16" "Gregor," "Blue Suit," Frido-Trendon Ltd., circa late-70s, $300.00.
Courtesy Dorisanne Osborn.

**16" early Gotz, "Sasha" dolls, showing the
two facial types and eye painting variations,
circa 1964 – 1970, $1,250.00+.**
Courtesy Dorisanne Osborn.

**Photo from Gotz Puppenfabrik 1996 brochure –
16" "Lilly," and 16" "Andrea" baby,
retail prices.**
Courtesy Dorisanne Osborn.

Shirley Temple

In 1934, after Shirley Temple stole the show with her performance in *Stand Up and Cheer,* Ideal gained the license to produce Shirley Temple dolls, hired Bernard Lipfert to sculpt a prototype, cast her in composition, and soon had Shirley Temple dolls in red and white polka dotted dresses on the market. The costumes were designed by Mollye Goldman during 1934 – 1936 and show the NRA markings on their labels. The costumes were sold separately as well as with the doll. The composition dolls had sleep eyes, with some flirty eyes, open mouth with six upper teeth, multi-stroke eyebrows, a five-piece jointed body, mohair wig, and soon came in a range of sizes from 11" to 27". The first dolls were packaged with a pinback button and signed photograph. Marked on the head and/or torso, with "SHIRLEY TEMPLE//IDEAL NOV. & TOY CO." and "SHIRLEY TEMPLE" on the body. In late 1935, a Shirley Temple Baby was introduced followed by baby carriages and accessories. The Shirley Temple dolls were popular through the early 40s, declining when Shirley reached adolescence.

In 1957, Ideal reissued a vinyl 12" Shirley to coincide with the release of her movies to television audiences and as Temple started her own television series. They have plastic script pins and paper hangtags. In the 1960s, 15", 17", and 19" vinyl dolls were issued. In 1972, Montgomery Wards, to celebrate its 100th anniversary, issued a 15" vinyl Shirley Temple. In 1982, Ideal made 8" and 12" Shirley Temple dolls costumed as Heidi, Stowaway, Stand Up and Cheer, The Little Colonel, Captain January, and The Littlest Rebel. Danbury Mint has made more recent Shirley Temple dolls, including porcelain 20" dolls costumed from movies, designed by Elke Hutchens. See Collectors' Network for information on several Shirley Temple publications and groups.

7" "Shirley Temple" all-composition, with bare feet, original dress, painted features, heavily molded hair, marked "Japan," $300.00.
Courtesy Marilyn Ramsey.

12" vinyl, Ideal "Shirley Temple" prototype,
very few made, 1974, $1,000.00+.
Courtesy Pamela Martinec.

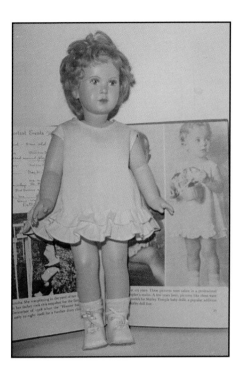

A very interesting composition "Shirley
Temple" portrait toddler by doll artist,
Dewees Cochran, $3,000.00+.
Courtesy Millie Busch.

18" composition, Ideal "Shirley Temple"
in "Scottie Dog" dress, boxed, $950.00.
Courtesy McMasters Doll Auctions.

16" composition, Ideal "Shirley Temple"
in pleated "Party Dress" with pin,
$900.00.
Courtesy McMasters Doll Auctions.

Shirley Temple

20" composition, Ideal "Shirley Temple" in "Music Note Dress," $600.00. *Courtesy McMasters Doll Auctions.*

25" composition, Ideal "Shirley Temple" in pleated "Party Dress," $675.00.
Courtesy McMasters Doll Auctions.

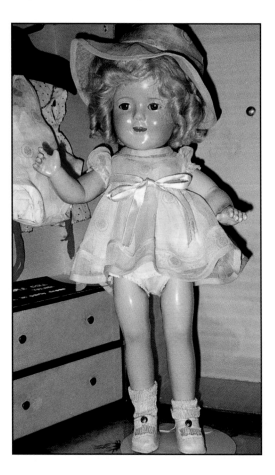

18" composition, Ideal "Shirley Temple" in pink pleated "Party Dress," boxed, $950.00.

Courtesy Iva Mae Jones.

16" composition, Ideal "Shirley Temple" in yellow "Stand Up and Cheer" outfit with trunk and wardrobe, $1,600.00.
Courtesy Iva Mae Jones.

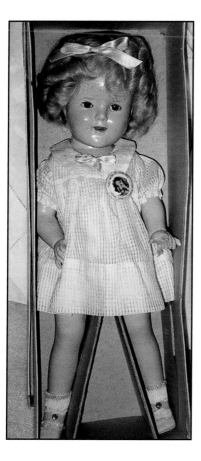

17" composition, Ideal "Shirley Temple" in shadow pane fabric dress, boxed, $875.00. *Courtesy Iva Mae Jones.*

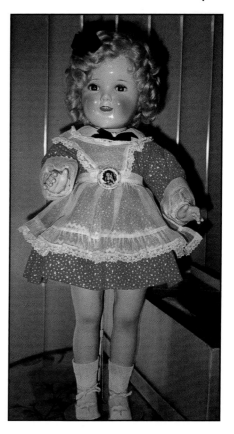

20" composition, Ideal "Shirley Temple" in red "Littlest Rebel" dress, boxed, $1,250.00.
Courtesy Iva Mae Jones.

18" composition, Ideal "Shirley Temple" in sailor "Captain January" outfit, $950.00. *Courtesy Rosemary Dent.*

16" composition, Ideal "Shirley Temple" in "Little Colonel" outfit, $900.00.
Courtesy Rosemary Dent.

Shirley Temple

18" composition, Ideal "Shirley Temple" in "Heidi" outfit, $1,800.00.
Courtesy Rosemary Dent.

11" composition, Ideal "Shirley Temple" in "Curly Top" outfit, $950.00.
Courtesy Iva Mae Jones.

18" composition, Ideal "Shirley Temple" dolls, each wearing pleated "Party Dresses," $950.00.

Courtesy McMasters Doll Auctions.

18" composition, Madame Alexander "Little Colonel," $1,000.00.
Courtesy McMasters Doll Auctions.

15" celluloid, marked with stork mark and "Shirley Temple," $400.00.
Unusual because of open crown and metal-type head covering,
dressed in Dutch type costume.
Courtesy Angie Gonzales.

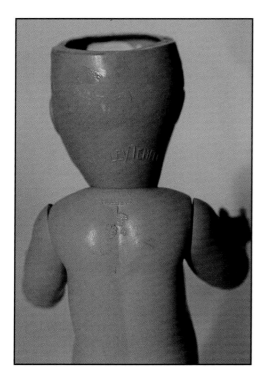

15" celluloid "Shirley Temple," back view
shows open crown, which is covered with a
metallic-type headdress, also shows stork
and "Shirley Temple" mark, $400.00.
Courtesy Angie Gonzales.

Shirley Temple

13" composition, Ideal "Shirley Temple" in "Little Colonel" outfit, all original, $725.00+.
Courtesy Rosemary Dent.

18" composition "Shirley Temple" in "Curly Top" outfit, pin, box, $950.00.
Courtesy Iva Mae Jones.

18" composition, Ideal "Shirley Temple" in "Curly Top" outfit, original aqua dress, button, $950.00.
Courtesy Rosemary Dent.

20" composition, Ideal "Shirley Temple" in aqua "Starburst" dress, $1,100.00.
Courtesy Rosemary Dent.

**18" composition, Ideal "Shirley Temple,"
made for Montgomery Wards 1939
Christmas season, all original, $950.00.**
Courtesy Glorya Woods.

**16" composition, Ideal "Shirley Temple
Baby," in tagged dress, $1,100.00+.**
Courtesy Rosemary Dent.

**13" composition, Ideal "Shirley Temple" in
tagged (NRA), pleated "Party Dress," pin,
box, $2,000.00.**
Courtesy McMasters Doll Auctions.

**36" vinyl, Ideal "Shirley Temple,"
original nylon dress, $1,100.00,
15" vinyl, Ideal "Shirley Temple" in original
"Wee Willie Winkie" outfit, $375.00.**
Courtesy McMasters Doll Auctions.

Shirley Temple

**18" composition, Ideal "Shirley Temple" in
original blue organdy dress, box, $1,300.00.**
Courtesy McMasters Doll Auctions.

**18" composition, Ideal "Shirley Temple"
original blue dress, trunk,
extra original outfits, $900.00.**
Courtesy McMasters Doll Auctions.

**13" composition, Ideal "Shirley Temple"
"Little Colonel" outfit, with more original
wardrobe, and trunk, $950.00.**
Courtesy McMasters Doll Auctions.

**16" composition, Ideal "Shirley Temple,"
original pleated "Party Dress," box,
$600.00.** *Courtesy McMasters Doll Auctions.*

**27" composition, Ideal "Shirley Temple,"
original "American Legion" outfit, box,
$1,200.00.**
Courtesy McMasters Doll Auctions.

**25" composition, Ideal "Shirley Temple,"
original "Stand Up and Cheer" dress,
box, $1,600.00.**
Courtesy McMasters Doll Auctions.

Signed promotional photo of Shirley Temple.
Courtesy Matrix.

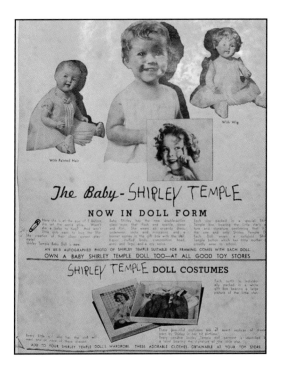

**Promotional material from original box
features "Baby Shirley," in the wigged and
unwigged versions.**
Courtesy Matrix.

13" composition "Shirley Temple" in "Little Colonel," costume with pin, box, clear eyes, lovely color, $750.00+.
Courtesy Matrix.

Close-up of 13" composition "Shirley Temple" in "Littlest Rebel," costume from the 1935 movie, $750.00+.
Courtesy Matrix.

13" composition "Shirley Temple," all original in "Littlest Rebel," costume and pin from the 1935 movie, $750.00.
Courtesy Matrix.

16" composition "Shirley Temple," all original with tagged "Curly Top," dress, pin, box, promotional material, circa 1934, $800.00+.
Courtesy Matrix.

Close-up of 16" composition "Shirley Temple," all original, with tagged "Curly Top" dress, pin, box, promotional material, circa 1934, $800.00+.
Courtesy Matrix.

Terri Lee

Terri Lee was made from 1946 to 1962, in Lincoln, NE, and Apple Valley, CA. Dolls were first made of composition, then hard plastic and vinyl. They had a closed pouty mouth, painted eyes, wigs, and jointed body. They were marked on torso "TERRI LEE" and the early dolls were marked "PAT. PENDING." See Collectors' Network for more information.

16" "Terri Lee," in train dress with five extra outfits in wardrobe trunk, with dog, $400.00.
Courtesy Sally McVey.

Terri Lee

16" hard plastic, all original "Terri Lee,"
in red and white "Heart Fund dress,"
$400.00.
Courtesy Sally McVey.

16" hard plastic "Terri Lee," original box,
with extra outfits, $430.00.
Courtesy McMasters Doll Auctions.

19" hard plastic "Terri Lee," boxed,
$275.00.
Courtesy McMasters Doll Auctions.

16" hard plastic "Terri Lee," $400.00.
Courtesy Cathie Clark.

16" hard plastic "Terri Lee," $400.00.
Courtesy Cathie Clark.

16" hard plastic "Terri Lee," synthetic wig, painted features, jointed neck, shoulders, hips, original dress, $325.00.
Courtesy Stephanie Prince.

183

Travel Dolls

A new trend in collectibles has emerged over the past few years, with the concept of the travel doll. This is a revival of an early concept of pocket dolls, small dolls that could be tucked into a pocket or bag and brought out when the child needed to be amused. Retired librarian, Adele Leurquin, while researching fashion articles in turn-of-the-century fashion magazines, came across an article about travel dolls. The doll was taken only on trips or excursions and put away when returning home. She brought the idea to her club and they all found small dolls and began sewing for them.

There are no hard and fast rules for the dolls, but some guidelines are mentioned. Travel dolls are usually small dolls so they can be easily carried. You may wish to choose a doll of the heights, 4½" to 9" tall. Your travel doll can be of any material, old or new, bisque, hard plastic, composition, vinyl, wood, or other material. It is nice if your travel doll has jointed legs so that she can sit without a doll stand when you take her to club meetings, luncheons, conventions, or on trips. It is nice to have a container such as a trunk or suitcase to carry your travel doll, her accessories, and wardrobe. Some have been quite creative when choosing trunks; Patches, a travel bear, makes his home in his own wooden "ammo" case.

It is fun to record your travel doll's experiences in a journal so that you can keep track of what is happening to her. This concept is just for fun, a way to be creative and express your own ideas without having to conform to any rules or regulations and is particularly enjoyed by those who like to create wardrobes. Travel dolls can have a new costume for each new trip to reflect where they have traveled. One travel doll received an Amish black hat, dress, and apron when she visited Pennsylvania. Travel doll trekkers provided their travel dolls with cowboy attire at a national doll convention recently in Dallas. Because the doll is small, it can be taken on extended trips in motorhomes, trains, or automobiles. This is a concept — so you can improvise with your own personal choices and it still remains a great idea for amusing a child (or an adult) when traveling.

7" travel doll created with new body, old bisque Kestner head marked "150,"
and a talented seamstress who made the entire wardrobe,
adding accessories as souvenirs of her travels, $1,000.00.
Courtesy Sue Kincade.

8" Vogue, hard plastic, painted lash, strung
"Ginny," all original with pink and black
box. This 8" doll makes a perfect size for a
travel doll, circa 1953, $325.00.
Courtesy Stephanie Prince.

Vinyl

By the mid-fifties, vinyl (polyvinylchloride) was being used for dolls. Soft material and processing that allowed hair to be rooted are positive attractions. Vinyl has become a desirable material and the market has been deluged with dolls manufactured from this product. Many dolls of this period are of little known manufacturers, unmarked or marked only with a number. With little history behind them, these dolls need to be mint in box and totally complete to warrant top prices. An important factor to remember when purchasing vinyl dolls: all aspects of originality, labeled costume, hang-tag, and box are more critical when these dolls are entered into competition.

13½" "Baby Face," by Galoob expressive character faces, rooted hair, jointed elbows and knees, set eyes, marked "C 1990 LGT 1/#3 China," $55.00+.
Courtesy Bev Mitchell.

**18" "Pamela," cloth body holds
cassette player, came with cassette and book,
extra outfits, made by World of Wonder, 1986,
$175.00.**
Courtesy Angie Gonzales.

**14" "Baby So Beautiful," set eyes, wigged
many combinations, retail $20.00 (less at
wholesale clubs).**
Courtesy Bev Mitchell.

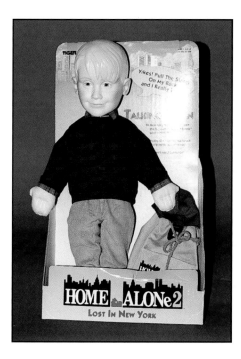

**18" talking "Kevin," from the movie
Home Alone 2, circa 1992, $50.00.**
Courtesy Angie Gonzales.

**12" "Michael Jackson,"
complete with box, circa 1984, $50.00.**
Courtesy Angie Gonzales.

17" Fisher Price "Mickie and Becky,"
with cloth bodies, circa 1980 – 1981, $50.00 each.
Courtesy Angie Gonzales.

11½" "Elizabeth Taylor,"
dressed in *Butterfield 8* costume,
$55.00.
Courtesy Cathie Clark.

Flagg flexible play dolls, family group, dollhouse dolls, $35.00.
Courtesy Cathie Clark.

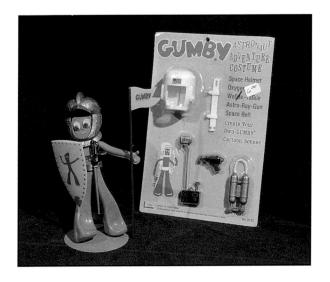

13" vinyl head, foam latex body reinforced with wire,
1965 Sears Catalog, sports figure, with wardrobe for
different sports, $75.00.
Courtesy Cathie Clark.

Character from animated cartoon, "Gumby,"
with Astronaut Adventure accessories, $25.00.
Courtesy Cathie Clark.

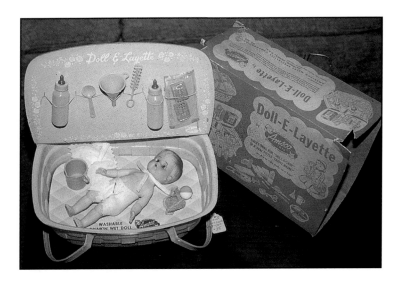

Late 1950s Amsco "Doll-E-Layette,"
in pink basket with accessories, $75.00.
Courtesy Cathie Clark.

"Staci," Dandee Doll Manufacturing,
circa 1978, $35.00.
Courtesy Cathie Clark.

Virga

Virga made hard plastic dolls jointed only at the arms and 7" dolls with inexpensive costumes sold as tourist dolls. In the 1950s, French designer Schiaparelli designed costumes for 12" Virga dolls with vinyl heads and hard plastic bodies. These dolls were marked "Virga" on the head and had a "Schiaparelli" tag in the skirt. Virga also made an 8" Go-Go with vinyl heads and hard plastic walker bodies with costumes by Schiaparelli, packed in shocking pink box.

**1950s "Virga Walking Doll," head turns
when she walks, $55.00.**
Courtesy Cathie Clark.

8" hard plastic "Playmates,"
box reads "A Virga Doll To Dress and Play;
The Perfect Doll To Share Your Day,"
$100.00.
Courtesy Cathie Clark.

8" hard plastic "My Name is Lucy, I walk," with wardrobe, $65.00.
Courtesy Cathie Clark.

Vogue

Jennie Graves started the company in the 1930s, in Medford, MA, and dressed Just Me dolls in early years. She also used dolls from Arranbee and had Bernard Lipfert design Ginny. After several changes of ownership, Vogue was recently purchased, in 1995, by the Wendy Lawton Company.

8" hard plastic "Ginny," $325.00.
Courtesy Marilyn Ramsey.

**8" hard plastic "Ginny," painted lashes,
$325.00.**
Courtesy Peggy Millhouse.

8" "Toddles," painted eyes, $400.00.
Courtesy Peggy Millhouse.

Ginny Playhouse, $1,000.00.
Courtesy Cathie Clark.

8" vinyl "Ginny," limited edition, from the Enchanted Doll House, $135.00.
Courtesy Iva Mae Jones

8" composition Oriental "Toddles," dressed in blue print kimono, with red flowers in her hair, $400.00+.
Courtesy Jackie Litchfield.

8" hard plastic "Ginny Bride" dolls, $350.00.
Courtesy Peggy Millhouse.

8" hard plastic "Ginny," $300.00.
Courtesy Peggy Millhouse.

**8" hard plastic "Ginny," in swimsuit,
with wardrobe, $250.00.**
Courtesy Candy McCain.

**8" hard plastic
"Ginny Bride," $275.00.**
Courtesy Connie Lee Martin.

**Left: 7½" composition "Toddles," with box, $270.00.
Right: 7½" hard plastic, painted-eye, "Ginny," with box,
$350.00.** *Courtesy McMasters Doll Auctions.*

**Composition "Uncle Sam"
and "Miss America Toddles," $450.00+.**
Courtesy Teri Pierce.

Vogue

16" vinyl "Miss Ginny," $45.00.
Courtesy Cathie Clark.

Advertising doll, "Cracker Jack," $85.00.
Courtesy Cathie Clark.

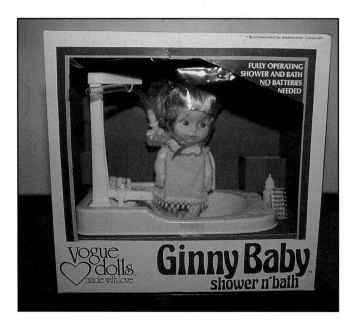

"Ginny Baby," with shower and bath, $75.00.
Courtesy Cathie Clark.

14½" vinyl "Littlest Angel," rooted hair, $125.00.
Courtesy Cathie Clark.

8" "Ginny Brides," $425.00 ea.
Courtesy Cathie Clark.

**Hard plastic "Ginny,"
and pup "Sparky," $400.00+.**
Courtesy Cathie Clark.

**8" hard plastic Ginny
"Brother and Sister, $450.00 ea.**
Courtesy Cathie Clark.

**8" hard plastic "Ginny,"
in cowboy outfit, $475.00.**
Courtesy Cathie Clark.

10" hard plastic "Jill" dolls,
advertised as Ginny's big sister, $175.00.
Courtesy Cathie Clark.

10½" hard plastic "Jill" dolls, high heel
fashion-type doll, big sister to Ginny,
circa 1957, $190.00 – 350.00.
Courtesy Cathie Clark.

10½" hard plastic "Jill" in
skating costume, $300.00.
Courtesy Cathie Clark.

Hard plastic "Jeff" dolls, friend of Jill,
circa 1957, $95.00+.
Courtesy Cathie Clark.

Hard plastic, "Jill,"
in skier costume, $350.00.
Courtesy Cathie Clark.

Jill's best friend is "Jan," hard plastic,
teen fashion dolls, $135.00.
Courtesy Cathie Clark.

Hard plastic, teenage fashion dolls "Jill,"
in fashion wardrobe, $350.00+.
Courtesy Cathie Clark.

With baby sister "Ginnette," was 8" baby brother,
"Jimmy," circa 1958, $65.00 ea.
Courtesy Cathie Clark.

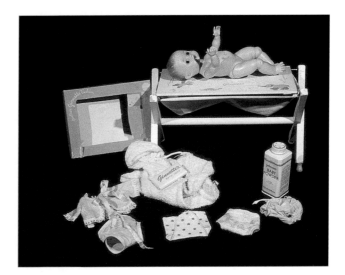

8" "Ginnette," Ginny's baby sister,
had large wardrobe, and accessories available,
circa 1958, $65.00+.
Courtesy Cathie Clark.

8" "Ginnette," Ginny's baby sister,
circa 1958, $65.00+.
Courtesy Cathie Clark.

Robin Woods

Beginning in the 1980s, Robin Woods was the creative designer for various companies, including Le Petit Ami, Robin Woods Company, Madame Alexander (Alice Darling), Horsman, and Playtime Productions. Robin Woods dolls cover a wide range of mediums, most of her early dolls are cloth. Great costuming is one factor that endears Robin Woods dolls to collectors.

14" vinyl "Amuse,"
Camelot Castle Collection, circa 1990, $125.00.
Courtesy Toni Winder.

**14" vinyl "Pollyanna,"
circa 1986, $175.00.**
Courtesy Toni Winder.

**18" cloth "Elizabeth," circa 1986,
$275.00.**
Courtesy Toni Winder.

**14" vinyl "Caroline & Her Carriage," Easter
Special, circa 1987, $150.00.**
Courtesy Toni Winder.

8" vinyl "Miss Muffet," circa 1991, $160.00.
Courtesy Toni Winder.

Robin Woods

14" vinyl "Becky visits the Farm," never in catalog, (rare), circa 1990, $150.00.
Courtesy Toni Winder.

14" vinyl "Krystal," This is my Country Series, circa 1990, $150.00.
Courtesy Toni Winder.

14" vinyl "Eliza Doolittle," circa 1990, $150.00.
Courtesy Toni Winder.

14" vinyl "Valentina," Valentine's Day special, circa 1987, $250.00.
Courtesy Toni Winder.

14" vinyl, hand-painted eyes, "Cinderella Ball Gown," circa 1987, $225.00.
Courtesy Toni Winder.

18" cloth "Polka Dot," circa 1986, $275.00.
Courtesy Toni Winder.

Robin Woods

18" cloth "Happy Holiday," circa 1985, $300.00.
Courtesy Toni Winder.

18" cloth "Love,"
limited edition of 1,000, $600.00.
Courtesy Toni Winder.

18" cloth "Clara," circa 1984, $275.00.
Courtesy Toni Winder.

**14" vinyl "William Noel,"
circa 1989, $150.00.**
Courtesy Toni Winder.

**14" vinyl "Merry Carol,"
circa 1988, $250.00+.**
Courtesy Toni Winder.

**14" vinyl "Elizabeth St. John," circa 1989,
$150.00.**
Courtesy Toni Winder.

**14" vinyl "Marcella," circa 1987,
$175.00.**
Courtesy Toni Winder.

Robin Woods

14" vinyl "Happy"
(1st one)," circa 1987, $250.00.
Courtesy Toni Winder.

14" vinyl "Little Queen Guinevere" Camelot Castle
Collection, circa 1988, $250.00.
Courtesy Toni Winder.

14" vinyl "Morgan Le Fey," Camelot Castle
Collection, circa 1988, $200.00.
Courtesy Toni Winder.

**14" vinyl "Chrissy," retailer's thank-you gift,
circa 1988, $350.00.**
Courtesy Toni Winder.

**9" vinyl "Nina,"
for Bea Skydell's Toys, circa 1988 – 1989, $300.00.**
Courtesy Toni Winder.

**14" vinyl "Angelina," J.C. Penney's
special, circa 1990, $200.00.**
Courtesy Toni Winder.

Robin Woods

**14" vinyl "Patti Marie," limited edition
of 250 for Disneyland, circa 1991,
$200.00.**
Courtesy Toni Winder.

**14" vinyl "Mitsy,"
limited edition for Disney World,
circa 1990, $225.00.**
Courtesy Toni Winder.

**9" vinyl "Tinkerbelle,"
special for Disney World, circa 1990,
$150.00.**
Courtesy Toni Winder.

14" vinyl "Audrey," limited edition of 500 for It's A Zoo, circa 1990 – 1991, $200.00.
Courtesy Toni Winder.

8" vinyl "Dee Dee," limited edition for Disney, circa 1996, $150.00.
Courtesy Toni Winder.

14" vinyl "Rainey," 1991 Robin Woods Club doll, $200.00.
Courtesy Toni Winder.

14" vinyl "Julianna Christina Penelope," limited edition for J.C. Penney's, circa 1991, $225.00+.
Courtesy Toni Winder.

Reference

No one person can know it all. With the passing of time, as more and more dolls come onto the market, more and more collectors are grouping together to share their interests and are specializing in one or more categories. These are dealers, clubs, or collectors who specialize in one category or type of doll who are willing to network with others. If you specialize in one of the categories listed in the price guide and want to share your knowledge with other collectors, please send us your specialty and references.

Collectors' Network

It is recommended that when contacting references below and requesting information that you enclose a SASE (self-addressed stamped envelope) if you wish to receive a reply.

Antique Dolls
Can research your wants:
Matrix
PO Box 1410
New York, NY 10023

Antique and Modern Dolls
Can research your wants:
Rosalie Whyel Museum of Doll Art
1116 108th Avenue N.E.
Bellevue, WA 98004
Phone: 206 455-1116
FAX 206 455-4793

Auction Houses
Call or write for a list of upcoming auctions or if you need information about selling a collection.
McMasters Doll Auctions
James and Shari McMasters
PO Box 1755
Cambridge, OH 43725
Phone 1-800-842-35226
Phone: 614-432-4419
FAX 614-432-3191

Barbies, Mattel
Jaci Jueden
3096 Williams Hwy
Grants Pass, OR 97527

Steven Pim
3535 17th St.
San Francisco, CA 94110

Celebrity Dolls
Celebrity Doll Journal
Loraine Burdick, Editor
413 10th Ave. Ct. NE
Puyallup, WA 98372
Quarterly, $10.00 per year

Composition and Travel Dolls
Effanbee's Patsy Family
Patsy & Friends Newsletter
PO Box 311
Deming, NM 88031
Bi-monthly, $20.00 per year

Costuming
Doll Costumer's Guild
Helen Boothe, Editor
7112 W. Grovers Ave
Glendale, AZ 85308
$16.00 per year, bimonthly

French Fashion Gazette
Adele Leurquin, Editor
1862 Sequoia SE
Port Orchard, WA 98366

Dionne Quintuplets
Quint News
Jimmy and Fay Rodolfos, Editors
PO Box 2527
Woburn, MA 01888

Quint Collector
Connie Lee Martin
4018 East 17th St.
Tucson, AZ 85711

Girl Scouts
Girl Scout Doll Collectors Patch
Pidd Miller
PO Box 631092
Houston, TX 77263

Girl Scout Dolls
Diane Miller
13151 Roberta Place
Garden Grove, CA 92643

Hitty
Friends of Hitty Newsletter
Virginia Ann Heyerdahl, Editor
2704 Bellview Ave
Cheverly, MD 20785
Quarterly, $12.00 per year

Jem Dolls, Hasbro
Linda E. Holton
P.O. Box 6753
San Rafael, CA 94903

Klumpe Dolls
Sondra Gast
PO Box 252
Spring Valley, CA 91976
FAX 619 444-4215

Lawton, Wendy
Lawton Collectors Guild
PO Box 969
Turlock, CA 95381

Toni Winder
1484 N. Vagedes
Fresno CA 93728

Liddle Kiddles
For a signed copy of her book,
Liddle Kiddles, $22.95 post pd., write:
Paris Langford
415 Dodge Ave
Jefferson, LA 70127
504-733-0676

Museums
Rosalie Whyel Museum of Doll Art
1116 108th Avenue N.E.
Bellevue, WA 98004
206 455-1116
FAX: 206 455-4793

Nancy Ann Storybook
Elaine Pardee
PO Box 6108
Santa Rosa, CA 95406
707 585-3655

Oriental Dolls
Ninsyo Journal
Japanese American Dolls Enthusiasts
JADE
406 Koser Ave
Iowa City, Iowa 52246

Repairs
Kandyland Dolls
PO Box 146
Grande Ronde, OR 97347
503-879-5153

Oleta's Doll Hospital
1413 Seville Way
Modesto, CA 95355
209-523-6669

Roldan Dolls
Sondra Gast
PO Box 252
Spring Valley, CA 91976
FAX 619 444-4215

Sandra Sue Dolls, Richwood Toys Inc.
Peggy Millhouse
510 Green Hill Road
Conestoga, PA 17516

Sasha Dolls
Friends of Sasha
(Quarterly Newsletter)
Dorisanne Osborn, Editor
Box 187
Keuka Park, NY 14478

Shirley Temple
Shirley Temple Collectors News
Rita Dubas, Editor
881 Colonial Rd
Brooklyn NY 11209
Quarterly, $20 year

Lollipop News
Shirley Temple Collectors by the Sea
PO Box 6203
Oxnard, CA 93031
Membership dues: $14.00 year

Terri Lee
Terri Lee Newsletter
Betty J. Woten
12 Big Bend Cut Off
Cloudcroft, NM 88317-9411

Woods, Robin
Toni Winder
1484 N. Vagedes
Fresno, CA 93728

Bibliography

Anderton, Johana
> *Twentieth Century Dolls*, Trojan Press, 1971
> *More Twentieth Century Dolls*, Athena Publishing Co. 1974

Axe, John
> *Effanbee, A Collector's Encyclopedia 1949 thru 1983*, Hobby House Press, 1983
> *The Encyclopedia of Celebrity Dolls*, Hobby House Press, 1983

Casper, Peggy Wiedman
> *Fashionable Terri Lee Dolls*, Hobby House Press, 1988

Coleman, Dorthy S., Elizabeth Ann and Evelyn Jane
> *The Collector's Book of Dolls Clothes*, Crown Publishers, 1975
> *The Colector's Encyclopedia of Dolls, Vol. I & II*, Crown Publishers, 1968, 1986

DeWein, Sibyl and Joan Ashabraner
> *The Collector's Encyclopedia of Barbie Dolls and Collectibles*, Collector Books, 1977

Garrison, Susan Ann
> *The Raggedy Ann & Andy Family Album*, Schiffer Publishing, 1989

Izen, Judith
> *A Collector's Guide to Ideal Dolls*, Collector Books, 1994

Judd, Polly and Pam
> *Hard Plastic Dolls*, Hobby House Press, 1987, 1994
> *Glamour Dolls of the 1950s & 1960s*, Hobby House Press, 1988

Langford, Paris
> *Liddle Kiddles*, Collector Books, 1996

Lewis, Kathy and Don
> *Chatty Cathy Dolls,* Collector Books, 1994

Mandeville, A. Glen
> *Ginny, An American Todller Doll*, Hobby House Press, 1994

Niswonger, Jeanne D.
> *That Doll Ginny*, Cody Publishing, 1978

Olds, Patrick C.
> *The Barbie Years*, Collector Books, 1996

Pardella, Edward R.
> *Shirley Temple Dolls and Fashions*, Schiffler Publishing, 1992

Schoonmaker, Patricia N.
> *Effanbee Dolls: The Formative Years, 1910 – 1929*, Hobby House Press, 1984
> *Patsy Doll Family Encyclopedia*, Hobby House Press, 1992

Smith, Patricia R.
> *Madame Alexander Collector Dolls*, Collector Books, 1978
> *Doll Values, Antique to Modern, Editions 1 – 12*, Collector Books
> *Modern Collector's Dolls, Series 1 – 8,* Collector Books

Index

Schroeder's
ANTIQUES
Price Guide

. . . is the #1 best-selling antiques & collectibles value guide on the market today, and here's why . . .

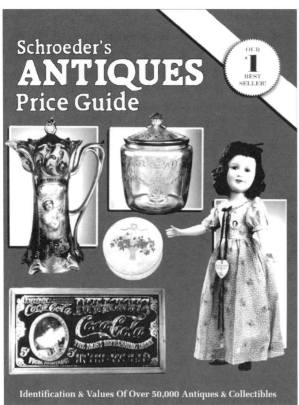

Identification & Values Of Over 50,000 Antiques & Collectibles

8½ x 11, 608 Pages, $12.95

• *More than 300 advisors, well-known dealers, and top-notch collectors work together with our editors to bring you accurate information regarding pricing and identification.*

• *More than 45,000 items in almost 500 categories are listed along with hundreds of sharp original photos that illustrate not only the rare and unusual, but the common, popular collectibles as well.*

• *Each large close-up shot shows important details clearly. Every subject is represented with histories and background information, a feature not found in any of our competitors' publications.*

• *Our editors keep abreast of newly developing trends, often adding several new categories a year as the need arises.*

If it merits the interest of today's collector, you'll find it in *Schroeder's*. And you can feel confident that the information we publish is up to date and accurate. Our advisors thoroughly check each category to spot inconsistencies, listings that may not be entirely reflective of market dealings, and lines too vague to be of merit. Only the best of the lot remains for publication.

Without doubt, you'll find
SCHROEDER'S ANTIQUES PRICE GUIDE
the only one to buy for
reliable information and values.

COLLECTOR BOOKS
A Division of Schroeder Publishing Co., Inc.